THE BEST OF
STAR WARS
INSIDER ®

TITAN

WWW.TITAN-COMICS.COM

THE BEST OF
STAR WARS
INSIDER

"A long time ago, in a galaxy far, far away...."

The epic saga of the Skywalkers has been thrilling
audiences all over the world since 1977.
A deceptively simple tale of good versus evil, it has
captured the imagination of generation after generation
as it has been passed down from fathers to sons,
and mothers to daughters.

Now, in this first special collection celebrating the greatest
space fantasy of all time, the best material from *Star Wars Insider*
magazine takes us back to a galaxy far, far away. Meet
the talented actors, crew members, artists, and writers who
have all played a part in the global phenomenon that is *Star Wars*.

CONTENTS

The Best of *Star Wars Insider*
Volume One
ISBN: 978-1-78585-116-2

Published by Titan
A division of Titan Publishing Group Ltd.,
144 Southwark Street,
London
SE1 0UP

© 2016 Lucasfilm Ltd. and ™
All Rights Reserved.
Used Under Authorised User.

Collecting material previously published in
Star Wars Insider Magazine.

No part of this publication may be reproduced, stored in a retrieval system, or transmitted, in any form or by any means, without the prior written permission of the publisher.

A CIP catalogue record for this title is available from the British Library.

First Edition March 2016
10 9 8 7 6 5 4 3 2 1

Printed in China.

Editor Jonathan Wilkins
Art Director Oz Browne
Acting Studio Manager Selina Juneja
Publishing Manager Darryl Tothill
Publishing Director Chris Teather
Operations Director Leigh Baulch
Executive Director Vivian Cheung
Publisher Nick Landau

Acknowledgments
Titan Would Like to Thank...
The cast and crew of *Star Wars* for giving up their time to be interviewed, and J. W. Rinzler and Pablo Hidalgo at Lucasfilm for all their help in putting this volume together.

MARK HAMILL
EXCLUSIVE INTERVIEW

STAR WARS INSIDER
AWARDS RESULTS ISSUE!

STAR WARS

INSIDER

EXCLUSIVE!
MARK HAMILL
on Luke, Lucas, and life!

ALSO INSIDE: *THE CLONE WARS,*
INDIANA JONES, AND MORE!

TITAN

ISSUE 137
Nov/Dec 2012
U.S. $7.99 CAN $9.99
Display Until 12/10/12

3 7 >

0 74808 01805 5

MARK HAMILL
LUKE SKYWALKER

ISSUE 137
NOVEMBER/DECEMBER 2012

Kids are often presented with stark choices as they grow up. In the school playgrounds of the late 1970s and early 1980s, the choice was between Han Solo and Luke Skywalker. The choice for me was very easy: From his amazing floating car to his cool black robes, I've always been a Luke fan.

Don't let anyone tell you different: Mark Hamill offers a consummate performance as Luke journeys from whiny brat to a powerful Jedi Knight. He helps sell the idea that Yoda is a Jedi Master as effectively as Frank Oz's stellar performance as Yoda. Not to take anything away from Oz, but if Luke didn't believe, *we* wouldn't believe. And it's fair to say that nobody believes in the magic of *Star Wars* more than Mark Hamill.

And he's a lovely guy, too. Great with fans, and hilarious to interview—he even punctuates fresh anecdotes with a friendly, "I've not told that story before!"

When *Insider* was offered the chance to publish unseen interviews with the three leads from the original trilogy, we leapt at the chance. Discovering later that they were the first *Star Wars* interviews was an added bonus. These discussions come from an almost unimaginable time when nobody knew what *Star Wars* was and the amazing effect it would have on all our lives.

Always wanting to be sure that our interview subjects are happy with the way in which they are presented—are *you* the same person you were nearly 40 years ago?—I took a chance meeting with Mark's wife and daughter, Marilou and Chelsea, at *Star Wars* Celebration VI in Florida to ask if he would like to check the material to see if there was anything he'd like to delete. Thankfully he was happy and intrigued at the idea of us publishing a piece of "ancient history." This led to Chelsea remarking, "You know, you really should do a new interview with my dad." But that, we will save for another time....—**Jonathan Wilkins**

Mark Richard Hamill was born on September 25, 1951. He is best known for portraying Luke Skywalker in the original Star Wars *trilogy (1977-1983), a role he reprised in* Star Wars: The Force Awakens *(2015). Hamill has forged a successful career as a voice actor, most notably supplying a fan favorite performance as the Joker in the* Batman *franchise; beginning with* Batman: The Animated Series *in 1992.*

BECOMING

LUKE

THE MARK HAMILL INTERVIEW BY CHARLES LIPPINCOTT

MARK HAMILL CHATS WITH CHARLES (CHARLEY) LIPPINCOTT, LUCASFILM VICE PRESIDENT OF MARKETING AND MERCHANDISING. LIKE THE CARRIE FISHER INTERVIEW, IT TOOK PLACE JUST MONTHS BEFORE THE *STAR WARS* PHENOMENON BEGAN, IN JANUARY 1977! IN THE INTERVIEW, HAMILL TALKS AT LENGTH ABOUT HIS YOUTH, THE FILM, AND LOTS OF GOOD STUFF, REFLECTING HIS THOUGHTS AND OPINIONS FROM OVER 35 YEARS AGO!....

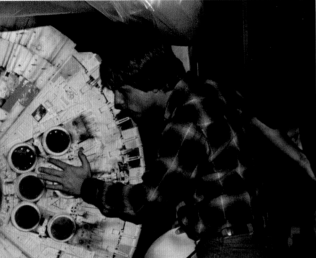

ON LUKE SKYWALKER AND JOINING THE *STAR WARS* CAST...

Mark Hamill: [Before joining the *Star Wars* cast], I wanted to be in *Apocalypse Now*. From what I understand, Fred [Roos, casting director] had a lot to do with guiding George Lucas in my direction. I think George did say he was doing a science fiction film.

Charley Lippincott: Had you seen George's *THX* at the time?

Hamill: No, but I had seen *American Graffiti* three or four times. I didn't see *THX* until after I had made *Star Wars*. I also saw the student film at a science fiction convention that we went to.

But I was amazed how perfectly constructed the story of *Star Wars* is. Luke grows up in *Star Wars*. He's thrown into this thing, but I think he learns a whole lot. There was also that romantic triangle. It's like Cary Grant, Rosalind Russell, and Ralph Bellamy in *His Girl Friday*. The two robots, Artoo-Detoo and See-Threepio, are like Laurel and Hardy. I love them. I think they are my favorite pair of characters.

As a human being, I enjoy Harrison's character, Han Solo, the most. But then I think Luke also emulates Harrison, so we're getting into how there are parallels between the cast and the storyline.

ON GARY KURTZ...

Hamill: Gary Kurtz (producer of *Star Wars*) is like Mr. Machine. He knows everything. I don't think I have ever asked Gary a question once that he couldn't answer. Gary and George are both so unique. You can't really compare them to any other producer-director you work with. Gary is a kid, too. The first time I really made a connection with Gary was in Tunisia. And he gets this excited little grin that he sort of suppresses and tells you all about Scrooge McDuck and the island of Pago Pago, or whatever.

He's really a partner with George. I've worked more closely with the producer on this than on anything. He's really accessible. They both are. You can walk up to them and ask them questions. There is no fear of intimidation there. There is not a power thing in it. We're all in it together. I think George is really flexible about letting me try things. I mean, a lot of times you wouldn't even tell him what you were changing and you would do things and he wouldn't say anything. Whether he knows you're doing it or not, I don't know. Probably.

He told me not to say "THX 1138" anymore. We were bringing in the Wookiee, he's handcuffed, and the guy says, "Where are you going with this thing?" And the line was something like, "It's a prisoner transferred from cell block...." And then lots of letters and numbers. I love in-jokes, so I said, "This is prisoner transfer from THX 1138." He came over and said, "Don't do that." But we did four more takes and by the end I was doing it again. I think I did it on one he printed! With explosions and everything else involved, I just kept doing it.

> "JUST FROM THE SCRIPT ALONE, I THOUGHT *STAR WARS* WAS A WINNER."

ON GEORGE LUCAS...

Hamill: I went into *Star Wars* with an amazing amount of respect for George. Just from the script alone, I thought *Star Wars* was a winner. You have that certain amount of anxiety before you make any movie. But there was a calmer atmosphere on *Star Wars* than any other thing that I've done. George is the kind of director where you think, *Gee, they're not saying anything to me!* But he was keeping his eye on everything going on the set. And then it turns out that they know so much. They put it together, and they know exactly what they are doing.

George gave me the nickname "The Kid." I had earned that nickname before George gave it to me, to the extent that the crew went out and made up a T-shirt with a silver star on it that said, "THE KID." I brought it to England with me; it was like the last couple of weeks of the film, when I wore it in.

I would do anything for George. I'd go paint his house. Seriously. He's great. I may never get to work with him again, who knows? He told me once that he wanted to not make features anymore, that he wanted to go back and make student movies. I'd be in those too!

ON HARRISON FORD...

Hamill: I learned a lot from Harrison. I think he's going to be amazing in this movie. He has a way of acting where you can see the process and use what you think can work for you. It's all in the way he hears information. And the way he listens. Harrison always called me "kid". He once left a message on the switchboard at EMI that Mr. Ford had called. So I said, Mr. Ford, this is Mr. Kid returning your call! That made Harrison laugh. It's always nice to make Harrison laugh, you know!

Lippincott: He makes you work at it, doesn't he?

Hamill: Carrie and I have already discussed how he's sort of judging you. You're aware of that.

ON SIR ALEC GUINNESS...

Hamill: I've worked with people before that I've always admired. Patricia Neal was maybe the closest. But Sir Alec is my favorite actor. I think there's nobody more versatile than he is. A lot of people can't identify him, he looks different in all of his movies. As a kid, I loved *The Lavender Hill Mob* and *The Ladykillers*. Those were my favorites. I was completely in awe of the guy. But he's so humble and so disinterested in himself, it's amazing. He doesn't consider himself an important figure in cinema. He doesn't like to talk about his movies, he doesn't think they are important, or that they'll last. He's more thrilled at getting nominated for his screenplay, for *The Horse's Mouth*. That was more important to him.

Lippincott: Peter Cushing has been limited to a certain genre.

Hamill: Yeah, he has, which is too bad. I loved him when he played Sherlock Holmes in *Hound of the Baskervilles*. I think he's been limited, not because of his ability, but because of the association with a type of film.

Opposite page, clockwise: Hamill and Harrison Ford rehearse the final scene of *Star Wars*; the team together one last time in *Return of the Jedi*; larking around behind the scenes on *Jedi* with Harrison Ford.

Above: Hamill and Sir Alec Guinness in Tunisia.

ON EARLY INTERESTS...

Hamill: I was always annoying people with magic tricks and puppets. My brothers and sisters would run away! My best trick was clearing the room in seven seconds. "Oh no! A new magic trick!" And they'd run in every direction. But I didn't tell a lot of people about my ambitions of working in movies, cause they just think you're nuts, especially when they don't work in this industry.

The only thing I never wanted to do was be in the circus, which I always thought was kind of eerie and creepy. A clown picked me up one time and scared me. He was up close and he just looked like a monster to me.

> ## "SIR ALEC GUINNESS IS MY FAVORITE ACTOR. THERE'S NOBODY MORE VERSATILE THAN HE IS."

Lippincott: Were you always interested in science-fiction movies?

Hamill: Yes. Fantasy science-fiction. In film, those were the big things. Ray Harryhausen movies, horror movies, and so on. *King Kong* was it for me, though, because I saw it at a very impressionable age.

I watched it five days in a row on the afternoon movies in New York. It used to just wipe me out every night. My parents told me I wasn't allowed to watch it the last couple of nights. I thought for some reason there was a chance of keeping Kong on the island and not taking him to civilization. I think that movie for me was what *Gone with the Wind* was for a lot of girls. It left me in a heap at the end.

I guess it was reading *Famous Monsters* magazine that I first realized at age seven or eight that this is a *job* for some people. That was it! I didn't know how, but secretly I always knew this is what I'd end up doing.

We weren't allowed to have comic books in my family. They were seen as a waste of money.... but we got them somehow. I had friends that had them. You could get your fix of monsters in *Classics Illustrated* there, you know, Frankenstein or whatever. I always loved comic books. I think that's why I love them so much now; I think I'm compensating for not being able to buy them then. I have a lot now, like Silver Surfer. I'm really fond of the DC heroes. I like Green Lantern. I love Superman. I really like Batman because of his mortality. I liked the vintage strips best of all.

I do remember being afraid to read EC horror comics. There would be comics like *Tales of The Crypt*, with somebody's eyeball hanging out. It was really hardcore. I like the EC Fantasy comics the best.

NOT JUST A JEDI
THE CAREER OF MARK HAMILL

Mark Hamill's diverse career as a performer has encompassed television, movies, and Broadway; more recently, he has enjoyed success as a writer, producer, and director.

He made his Broadway debut in the title role of *The Elephant Man*. He then played Mozart in the first National Tour of *Amadeus*.

Hamill's film credits include *The Big Red One, Brittania Hospital, Slipstream, Village of the Damned, Walking Across Egypt, Jay and Silent Bob Strike Back,* and *Comic Book: The Movie* (which he directed, co-wrote, and produced).

His voice can be heard in over 100 cartoons, including: *Batman: The Animated Series* (Annie Nomination Best Actor), *The Adventures of Batman and Robin, The Simpsons, Ren & Stimpy, Robot Chicken, Superman, Justice League, Spider-Man, Hulk, Powerpuff Girls,* *The Flintstones, Scooby Doo, Wizards, Batman: Mask of Phantasm,* and *Batman Beyond: Return of the Joker* (Annie Nomination Best Actor).

He reprised the voice of the Joker in the hit videogame, Arkham Asylum and gave a BAFTA award-winning performance in the sequel, Arkham City.

A devoted comic book collector and historian, Hamill has written for *The Simpsons* comic. His 20 year stint as the voice of the Joker remains a fan favorite, as are his two appearances as the villain The Trickster on *The Flash* television series.

He created the comic book anti-hero, *The Black Pearl* for Dark Horse Comics, which he co-wrote with Eric Johnson as a five-issue mini-series. A film adaptation is on the way.

Hamill is currently working on *Metalocalypse, Regular Show,* and *Disney's Motor City,* and *Dragons: Riders of Berk.*

He can be seen in *Sushi Girl,* out now on DVD and Blu-ray.

THE HERO'S JOURNEY

LUKE SKYWALKER'S PATH TO GREATNESS

1. TAKING CHARGE

We're not suggesting that Luke's plan to rescue the Princess on the first Death Star wasn't flawed, but the fact that the young farmboy manages to persuade Han and Chewie to go along with his plan— that's impressive.

2. TAKING DOWN THE DEATH STAR

He might have started as a whiny teenager, but Luke more than hints at his future potential as he proves that he really isn't such a bad pilot and possibly even as good as his mysterious father....

3. RUMBLINGS OF THE FORCE

It's easily overlooked, but the first sense of Luke using the physical force can be seen as he races to collect his lightsaber from its icy home as a ferocious and very hungry wampa approaches at speed....

4. FACING VADER

Taking on the Dark Lord would be a brave move for even a vet-eran Jedi, but for an impatient Padawan? Thankfully, Luke's enough of a Jedi to hold his own, until Vader overwhelms him.

5. A JEDI AT LAST

During the daring battle at the Saarlac pit, Luke shows off his lightsaber skills in combat, in one of the many punch-the-air moments in the saga!

4

ON GROWING UP....

We moved around a lot. My earliest memory is around when we were living in San Francisco, then Virginia, then back to San Jose, Redwood City, then to Pennsylvania, then New York, then San Diego, then back to Virginia, then I went to spend the summer with my old family in San Francisco.

So my parents kept throwing things away without our knowledge. You would get to the next stop and say, "Hey whatever happened to my Cantinflas marionette (a Mexican comic film actor)?" And you'd discover it was given to charity.

"LIVING IN JAPAN WAS MY BEST FILM-GOING EXPERIENCE ANYWHERE. WE SAW ALL THE MOVIES FOR FREE!"

I'm right in the middle. I have two older sisters and an older brother and two younger sisters and a younger brother. We are spaced two or three years apart. We'd drive to the beach in two cars and discover that there were two people missing. And have to go back! "Well, I thought you had them." There they would be on the front doorstep in tears!

Then I went to Japan, where we stayed for almost three years. I finished 11th and 12th grade there. I graduated from Yokohama High.

Lippincott: Were there all American students?

Hamill: It was mostly Japanese, but it was an American speaking school. That was my greatest film-going experience anywhere. My father was in the navy and they had all the movies for free, and they were first run. They even had movies that were unreleased in theaters here. Plus foreign product, because the movies changed almost every night: you'd have no advance publicity. There'd be *Bonnie and Clyde*, color, 90 minutes, Warren Beatty and Faye Dunaway, crime and melodrama. That's all you'd know. I wish I could do that now with films. I'd like to just go and not know anything about it.

We also got to see the Japanese versions of movies. *The Good, The Bad and The Ugly* was a lot more violent and it had subtitles up and down the sides.

The Hammer films were gorier. Never dubbed, though. The Japanese films were never dubbed unless they were on television.

I think that *Star Wars* is going to be amazing there. The Japanese are film people. They love movies and they love

5

American movies, and they love science fiction. That's their whole Saturday morning TV thing. They've got *Astro Boy*, *Ultraman*, and all those great stars of Toho cinema. And even the second string characters, like Gedra and Gamara are great. There's a turtle that spins around and shoots fire out of his legs!

I tested for the voice of Astro Boy. I was in the finals and kept forgetting that it was all (*Mark does a nasal falsetto*) up here, you know? Not that, but more (*Mark's voice goes all breathy*) like this. You know how they talk in Japanese movies. (*In a rapid and slightly clipped accent*) "Oh. It must be Godzilla." I didn't get the job, but I was down there at the studio and saw big monster feet and little Japanese cities waiting to be crushed. I think the Japanese are going to go bananas for *Star Wars*.

Lippincott: What is the Japanese fascination with these kinds of movies?

Hamill: They like things that are way beyond their control. There's no way to really relate to Godzilla coming to step on your house! The Universal monsters of the 30s were humanoid, at least. You could run from the Mummy, if you didn't get too terrified and keep falling down all of the time, like Evelyn Ankers did. The Wolfman was pretty hardcore. He's fast, crazy and he bites you. But Frankenstein's monster is kind of a schlump. He just clogs along. You figure as a kid, unless you're so scared you can't get out of his way....

Lippincott: What was your life in Japan like?

Hamill: The most fun I ever had in my life. You have total independence. The trains and buses are cheap. You can travel really easily. And within the confines of the Naval base, it's a totally protected environment. If you are living in suburbia, you can't go out after a certain time, and you can't drive anyway. On the base, there's no fear of crime. There were so many activities. There was a teen club. They showed movies, there were pool tables and there were dances. There was even night-time miniature golf.

Just hanging out with friends was fun. You could just get on the free station-bus to opposite parts of the base. They wouldn't let you into the movies if your hair was over two inches or something, they'd measure it on the way in!

I did lots of plays there and stuff....

THE MANY OUTFITS OF LUKE SKYWALKER

FARMBOY CHIC

RATING: ✪✪✪✪✪

X-WING PILOT

RATING: ✪✪✪✪✪

They had a lot of facilities and playhouses and they would pay and you would get professional sets and so I went. We did *The Odd Couple* at school. It sounds funny because I probably had a real high voice! You can train bears to do that show and it would get laughs.

We did that show at school and it was so funny that they let us tour. They got us a big van and we went around and did it at officers' clubs. I've done that show more than any other show I've ever done. We must have done it 20 or 30 times.

I was really sad to leave Japan. As sorry as I was to find out I was going there. That was like being sentenced to going to Siberia. You're in the middle of high school —and you discover you're going to spend two years in Japan. I just didn't know what it would be like. You know, cause we thought we were really cool in Anandale, Virginia.

Lippincott: Had it changed that radically?

HOTH GEAR

RATING: ✦✦✦✦✦

BESPIN FATIGUES

RATING: ✦✦✦✦✦

JEDI THREADS

RATING: ✦✦✦✦✦

Hamill: Well, it did. For a month, I just hated the school. I thought everybody was just stupid and square and I was a loner, and that's how I started falling in with a "bad crowd," which is funny, because compared to hoods in existence now, these guys are tame. And I was the court jester. I was never a greaser or a fighter, and I would sit at their table and I was not allowed to be beat up by football players because these guys would then turn around and stick a monkey wrench up your nose because they were real scary.

In other words: when I sat with all of these hoods, that was my job. I would make them laugh, or whatever. Which is funny because I had never smoked marijuana or whatever or pills, anything like that. No, sir. And in my junior year, I remember looking back and thinking, *Oh, my god, those guys were really loaded.* I would go to their house and they'd be playing The Doors with the lights down and funny lights, and the incense and everything, and I was on a roll. I was thinking I'm the funniest man who ever lived....

Cause these guys would be hysterical.... And then I look back and think, *I'm sure they were loaded.* But I was their mascot, so to speak, which was great protection. ✦

┌─ **EXPANDED** ─────────

Follow Mark on Twitter
at @HamillHimself

──────────── **UNIVERSE** ─┘

JAMES EARL JONES
THE VOICE OF DARTH VADER

ISSUE 118
JULY/AUGUST 2010

Although he was originally uncredited for his work on *Star Wars* and *The Empire Strikes Back*, James Earl Jones' performance as the voice of Darth Vader is the perfect marriage of physical performance, costume, sound effects, and vocal performance, creating what is easily *Star Wars'* most iconic character. A modest man, Jones deemed his performance as just "special effects" until he became identified with the role and allowed himself to be credited.

He was brought in to replace David Prowse's heavy West Country accent, which, though it served as an on-set guide, was at odds with the menacing look of Vader. Until very late in the post-production process, George Lucas was convinced the character wouldn't work... until Jones' rich tone cemented the separate elements together. Jones reprised the role in *Revenge of the Sith* and later, *Star Wars Rebels*.

A multi-award-winning actor, Jones delighted fans when he played himself in an episode of *The Big Bang Theory* entitled "The Convention Conundrum," proclaiming to awestruck fan, Sheldon Cooper, "You love *Star Wars*? I love *Star Wars* too!"—**Jonathan Wilkins**

James Earl Jones was born in Arkabutla, Mississippi, on January 17, 1931. Over a career spanning more than 60 years he has become one of the most well-respected and best-loved actors working today.

Making his Broadway debut in 1957, Jones has won many awards, including a Tony Award and Golden Globe Award for his role in The Great White Hope. *He was also recognized at the Emmys, taking home three (two in the same year in 1991). He earned an Academy Award nomination for Best Actor in a Leading Role in the film adaptation of* The Great White Hope.

In 1994, he won a whole new audience with his vocal performance as Mufasa in Disney's The Lion King.

THE VOICE OF JAMES JONES

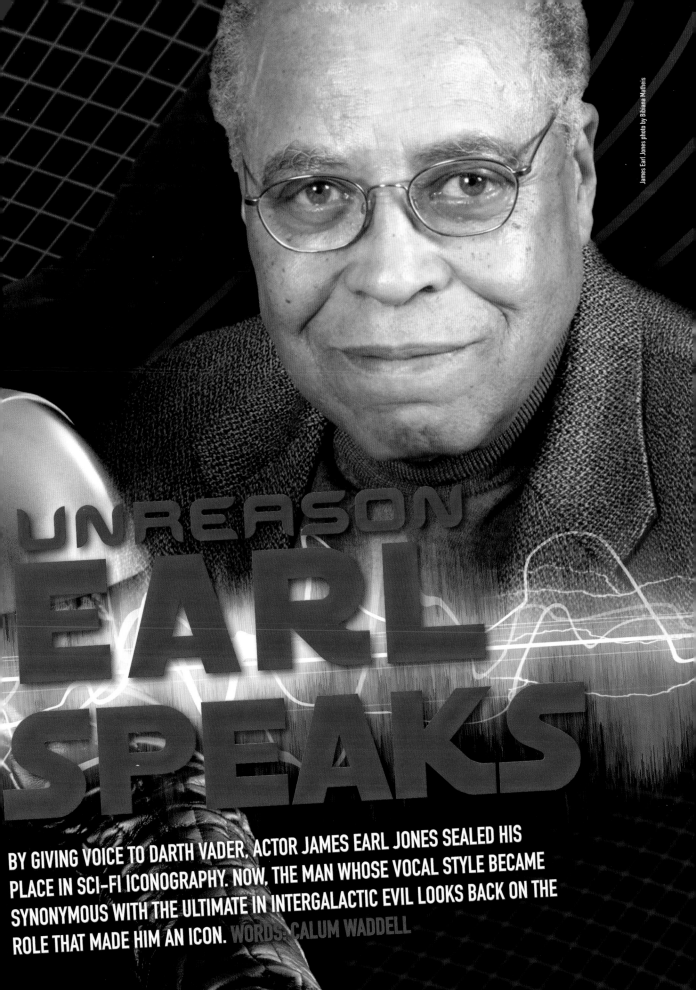

UNREASON
EARL
SPEAKS

BY GIVING VOICE TO DARTH VADER, ACTOR JAMES EARL JONES SEALED HIS PLACE IN SCI-FI ICONOGRAPHY. NOW, THE MAN WHOSE VOCAL STYLE BECAME SYNONYMOUS WITH THE ULTIMATE IN INTERGALACTIC EVIL LOOKS BACK ON THE ROLE THAT MADE HIM AN ICON. WORDS: CALUM WADDELL

As the voice of the world's most famous cinematic villain, James Earl Jones—now 79 years old—has, for an entire generation of movie buffs, become inseparable from *Star Wars*. Of course, as most readers know, the actor's illustrious career has spanned nearly five decades, beginning with a small turn in Stanley Kubrick's classic 1964 farce *Doctor Strangelove*, and includes a Best Actor Oscar nomination in 1970 for his role in the adaptation of the stage classic, *The Great White Hope*. Furthermore, additional turns in such blockbusters as *Conan the Barbarian* (1982), *Coming to America* (1988), and *The Hunt for Red October* (1990) have succeeded in making Jones one of the most identifiable thespians of recent times.

Recently the performer returned to his self-proclaimed "first love": the theatre, treading the boards six days a week in the London production of *Cat on a Hot Tin Roof*. Inevitably, this sort of schedule keeps the screen legend busy—although, during his appearance at the annual Glasgow Film Festival as the 2010 guest of honor, he conceded that he never actually had much of a career plan in mind. "I am what you would call a journeyman actor," he begins. "All my life I just took whatever

work came along to me. I am actually a little sorry to admit that I never had any big career goals. Maybe I should have because if you want to be an actor you really need to have all of your marbles together. But I have been lucky to get away with that and I still continue to work that way."

Perhaps unsurprisingly, it was this nonchalant attitude that led Jones to what is probably his most widely-known role. However, somewhat surprisingly, at first the actor was hesitant to admit that it was *his* voice that breathed life into everyone's favorite dark-caped, helmet-clad galactic bad guy. Despite being uncredited on both 1977's *A New Hope* and 1980's *The Empire Strikes Back.* (he finally lent his name to the closing credit scroll of 1983's *Return of the Jedi*) few hardened film buffs could fail to recognize the distinctive, deep-throated growl of Jones on the *Star Wars* soundtrack. Consequently, the actor noted that his initial decision not to reveal himself as the voice of Darth Vader had nothing to do with secrecy. "I was basically hired as a special effect," he says. "Dave Prowse was the guy acting as Darth Vader, okay? Why take that away from him?" A gentlemanly comment, certainly, and Jones also revealed that when he signed on to do *Star Wars* he opted to take the offer of a flat fee instead of a cut of the box-office take. In retrospect, that wasn't his best move. "I got paid $7,000," he laughs. "Now, that was for only two hours work. So to me that was like I was rolling in a bunch of clover. Of course, at the time, I did not know that if I had asked for percentage

"I AM VERY PROUD THAT I WAS A PART OF THE *STAR WARS* MOVIES!"

points of the gross, I would have been a millionaire overnight."

The actor noted that nobody involved in the original classic had any idea that it was going to be as big as it became, even its creator. "I did not expect *Star Wars* to become such a phenomenon and nor did George Lucas," he smiles. "The British crew who worked at Elstree Studios in London never knew either." In fact, it's well-established that much of the UK crew believed they were working on a B-movie that would come and go without much notice.

"I wouldn't go so far as to describe their attitude as being full of disdain, but there was a sense of 'Oh this is just a bunch of Americans making some kids' stuff,'" Jones says. "No one appreciated what it could be. When it did become

huge, it was largely because of kids. It was a movie for young people. But then I guess everybody stopped and thought about what we must have done right, including the voice of Darth Vader. And that led to the sequels!"

Happy to once again lend his vocal talents to *The Empire Strikes Back*, Jones said that his second time around was, in at least one way, an even more surreal experience. "I had always heard that David Prowse had a Scottish accent," he says. "I then discovered he was from Bristol. Now, if you cannot imagine Darth Vader with that kind of accent let me tell you *this* little story. By the time we did the second episode David Prowse knew that it was not going to be his voice. So he just read the words in a kind of monotone. So the director, Irvin Kershner, decided to lay his own voice over the soundtrack. He thought that would give me an idea of how the character should evolve. Now Irvin's voice is very high pitched and squeaky. Believe it or not, it is quite intimidating! I remember thinking, *Now this could be a very scary version of Darth Vader*!"

Naturally, being a big part of one of the most popular film franchises in history hardly hindered the actor's career. In fact, as Jones happily says, it introduced him to a new, lucrative career in voiceovers and villainous turns. "As soon as *Star Wars* hit I got offered a lot of commercials," he reveals. "Everyone saw it, of course, and then I got a call from the promotions department at Chrysler— the car manufacturer. They explained to my agent that they had designed a car called The Laser—and it had dark windows and a dark paint job so, of course, they wanted a dark voice promoting this thing! They even mentioned that they had Darth Vader in mind. So *Star Wars* opened up a whole new career for me."

Long-time Lucas acquaintance John Milius was certainly taken by *Star Wars* when he opted to cast Jones as the evil warlord Thulsa Doom in *Conan the Barbarian*. "Milius was a great script doctor and for *Conan* he collected a lot of speeches that had been given by famous tyrants," the actor reflected. "I think he had everything that was said

"I WAS BASICALLY HIRED AS A SPECIAL EFFECT!"

by every tyrant that ever existed, from Shaka Zulu to Hitler and just about anyone else you can name. He asked me to read them all and I was yelling down this canyon on the set in Southern Spain, delivering all of these real-life speeches. It was worth it, though. It helped to develop the character."

Although reticent about speaking out on *Star Wars* in the past, Jones says that he could not be happier with being involved in the series. "I am very proud that I was a part of them," he beams. "I am just glad that I can say I was a little piece of that success, in any way

"*STAR WARS* OPENED UP A WHOLE NEW CAREER FOR ME."

at all." However, he admitted that the awesome presence of Darth Vader is sometimes difficult to escape. "Most people, when they see me, want me to sign something to do with *Star Wars*," he confirms. "But there are a lot of other roles that I cherish and I want

people to see. I think that my favorites are *Cry, the Beloved Country*—which was a flop, unfortunately—*A Family Thing*, and *Field of Dreams*. I love having someone come up to me and, instead of asking me to sign a Darth Vader poster, remind me of a movie that I have completely forgotten. It just warms me. I like to say, 'Thank you for remembering that.'"

Despite lending his voice to the Galactic Empire's supreme warrior, Jones began life with a stutter that once threatened to curtail his acting ambitions. "I suppose that I am a walking irony in a way," he says. "But there are a lot of people who have been born with a weak muscle and by exercising that muscle it became their strongest point. I suppose when you think about it, becoming Darth Vader—after having had a stutter—is a little ironic but, like I say, I'm very proud of being a part of *Star Wars* movies. Very proud indeed."

STAR WARS
INSIDER

STAR WARS 30

LEGACY

STAR INTERVIEWS: MAKING *STAR WARS* IN THEIR OWN WORDS!

PLUS: DISCOVER THE *STAR WARS* EFFECT!
MEET THE FALL GUY: STUNTMAN PETER DIAMOND
THIRTY YEARS OF *STAR WARS* MEMORIES!
ALL THE LATEST *STAR WARS* GEAR REVEALED!

ISSUE #69 JULY/AUGUST 2007
$14.95(AUS)/$18.90(NZ)

CELEBRATING 30 YEARS OF THE GREATEST SPACE SAGA OF THEM ALL!

ANTHONY DANIELS & KENNY BAKER

C-3PO AND R2-D2

ISSUE 94

JULY/AUGUST 2007

Anthony Daniels has always made time to be interviewed for *Star Wars Insider*. One instance when I did get to speak with him was at a press line-up at Celebration in Essen, Germany. It can be difficult to come up with new lines of enquiry, and asking him "What was it like wearing the Threepio suit?" would have probably filled him with the same amount of dread as it filled me. Instead, I opted to ask him about working with the author Brian Daley on the much-loved National Public Radio (NPR) adaptations of the original *Star Wars* trilogy. Daniels lit up as he talked about his work on the plays, full of praise for Daley's writing.

A born entertainer, Kenny Baker's many talents include singing, dancing, acting, and being a virtuoso harmonica player. He's always fun to interview, with plenty to say about the challenges he faced while on the blisteringly hot *Star Wars* set in Tunisia, and his long and varied career working with Jim Henson, Terry Gilliam, Miloš Forman, and David Lynch.—**Jonathan Wilkins**

Born in Salisbury, England, on February 21, 1946, **Anthony Daniels** *studied law for two years, before heading for the National Theatre of Great Britain at The Young Vic. A meeting with George Lucas led to Daniels accepting the part of C-3PO, the prissy droid who would be a pivotal character throughout the entire* Star Wars *saga.*

A loyal ambassador of Star Wars, *Daniels is a regular attendee of the* Star Wars *Celebration conventions, as well as numerous promotional events in support of the saga.*

Born on August 24, 1934 in Birmingham, England, **Kenneth George "Kenny" Baker**'s *path to fame saw him join a circus, learn to ice skate, and join a troupe of performing dwarfs before forming a comedy group called the Minitones with his friend, and future* Star Wars *co-star, Jack Purvis.*

ANTHONY DANIELS
& KENNY BAKER
C-3PO & R2-D2

ANTHONY DANIELS AND KENNY BAKER ARE FOREVER LINKED AS THE ROBOT DUO WHO APPEARED IN ALL SIX *STAR WARS* MOVIES, EVEN THOUGH BOTH HAVE ENJOYED A VARIETY OF CHALLENGING ROLES OVER THE YEARS.

ANTHONY DANIELS ON C-3PO'S COSTUME

The gold suit looks big because it's glossy and shines. It gives the impression of greater stature. I spent some months at Elstree with a team of plasterers and a lovely sculptor called Liz Moore. First, they covered every part of me in Vaseline and then cling-film. Then they slopped plaster all over me. It was a rather disgusting experience...

Eventually, they put together this rather unattractive statue of me, cast from molds they created. Then, with clay, Liz built up the design you recognize on the screen. She was terrific, but it wasn't until I saw a Polaroid picture of myself on the first day's shooting in Tunisia that I really knew what I was playing for the next 12 weeks.

It was made up of about 16 pieces, on a good day: aluminum, plastic, fibreglass, rubber, cardboard and me. The trouble was that they didn't all quite fit together as intended. Being in the middle, so to speak, it seemed to be me that had to give in. I was fairly traumatized just by the two hours it took to dress on the first day. Even before we began the film, I was ready to go home. I think my dressers and helpers felt the same way but it did get better, especially in the other movies.

KENNY BAKER ON LIFE INSIDE R2-D2

There's just an opaque window, about four inches at the most in diameter and I couldn't see much at all. I didn't need to, as long as I could see who I was supposed to be reacting to. I'm moving my head from one side to the other to follow the gist of the conversations. That was about it really. I didn't walk anywhere, because they used the three-legged remote-controlled robot to move around. My costume weighs about 80 pounds. It's quite heavy, and I couldn't physically move it, apart from wobbling and jerking around and moving the head.

I'm acting away inside this thing. You just have to act through the costume. You're still doing the facial expressions, and whatever you need to do, making noises, to try to give the character some life.

I've done that quite often over the years in different costumes. It's the way I move, I presume. I've been told it's much more effective when I'm in R2-D2, as opposed to the remote-controlled robot. It's a robot; it doesn't really wobble and jiggle around, does it? Although it moves, it's static in other respects. It's a natural movement of the robot that they want to see, and then that's coupled with the dialogue and with the sound effects, and eventually George gets what he wants.

It's hard to know what he does want at times because you're doing what you're supposed to be doing and hoping it fits in with what's going on around you. You don't see much and you can't hear much, because of the enormous sound of the whirling of the lights and stuff inside the head of the robot. There are quite a few electronics going on inside there. You're slightly cut off from what's going on around you. But it seems to work.

ANTHONY DANIELS ON HIS DISTINCTIVE C-3PO VOICE

I spoke the lines as we filmed each scene. I had a tiny radio mike tucked into my left eyebrow. Wires ran over my head and right down my back, connecting it to a transmitter shoved in the only space available. Well, I couldn't sit down, anyway. I know quite a few people who talk out of the end of their anatomy!

The resulting tracks were fairly unintelligible. They picked up all the clanks and squeaks of the costume and especially my heavy breathing.

So after each take, minus costume, I would re-record the lines on the spot, to save the sanity and ears of the editor. I never realized that George Lucas would return to the States and search for another voice. I had sort of invented the personality the way I interpreted the script, but it wasn't quite what George had in mind. It was his film so I guess he could have anyone he wanted. Somehow, it didn't work with anyone else and eventually they flew me over to dub my voice onto the edited film. I've always looked after Threepio. Maybe, this time, he was looking after me.

It is my voice with a tiny amount of echo added to make it sound slightly tinny. I do talk a little differently from my normal voice. It's just that I feel a bit self-conscious talking like Threepio unless I'm in the suit. Rehearsing on set was always a little strange. Luke and Han sound like Mark and Harrison on set or in the bathroom, but I had to accept that talking as Threepio, I did leave myself open to one or two odd looks, especially from Harrison.

KENNY BAKER ON HIS *STAR WARS* EXPECTATIONS

Star Wars was just another film, as far as we were concerned at the time. It was nothing special. Nobody expected it to be something terrific. I thought if Alec Guinness was in it, it must have some credibility. He must know more than I do! Nobody thought it was going to be any good.

It was very confusing with Obi-Wan Kenobi and all these weird, funny names that you'd never heard of before, which at the time were hard to get your tongue around. The kids got them quickly but as usual the adults thought, "What the heck's all this about?"

ANTHONY DANIELS ON WORKING WITH ALEC GUINNESS

I don't think I could have played the role without his kindness and support.

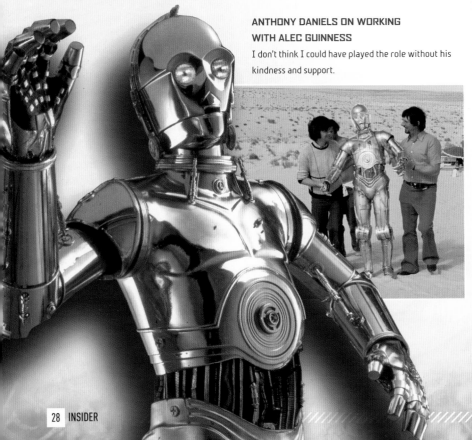

KENNY BAKER ON MARK HAMILL

He would come in with the boys and have a drink with everybody. Jack (Purvis) and I would take him out with us at night on the cabaret circuit in London, and show him what we did for our bread and butter.

ANTHONY DANIELS ON ACTING IN THE SUIT

One of the reasons I was offered the part all those years ago is that I was reasonably good at mime. They thought that an actor without that skill might just seize-up in a costume like that. In fact I can walk almost normally in the suit, in spite of the weight, but it doesn't look very interesting. So I developed a sort of shuffle, which did two things. First, it looked right for the character and secondly it kept my center of gravity right in the center. Otherwise, I would have lumbered around like a bantha. I had to experiment to see what kind of performance I could get through the suit. It severely restricted my gestures. I admit that showing any kind of emotion wasn't easy, but perhaps it worked sometimes. I was usually slightly cold in the desert scenes in Tunisia: we went from summer to winter conditions on an hourly basis. The crew did quick changes between T-shirts and parkas. I didn't have a change of clothes. The air was quite sharp and the suit reflected all the sunshine away from me.

ANTHONY DANIELS ON R2-D2

The problem was that he never spoke at all. In any scene with him I'd have to imagine what he said and reply to it. I'd leave some gaps for him. Makes it a bit hard to remember a scene sometimes. I asked George to say "beep" when I'd finished a speech and it was Artoo's turn to speak, but he was hopeless so I did it on my own. At the first screening of *Star Wars* I was amazed to hear what Ben Burtt had added as Artoo's voice. I'd never heard him before. 🌀

THE PHANTOM MENACE ATTACK OF THE CLONES THE EMPIRE STRIKES BACK RETURN OF THE JEDI
EPISODE I EPISODE II EPISODE V EPISODE VI

RALPH MCQUARRIE
ON DROIDS, VADER, AND MORE....

ATTACK POSITIONS!
THE X-WINGS: BACK IN BATTLE!

STAR WARS
INSIDER

VIDEOGAMES!

INSIDER CELEBRATES 30 YEARS OF DIGITAL ACTION!

ISSUE 135
AUG/SEPT 2012
Display until 09/04/2012
U.S. $6.99 CAN $7.99

TITAN

RALPH MCQUARRIE
CONCEPTUAL ARTIST

ISSUE 135
AUGUST/SEPTEMBER 2012

The difficult process George Lucas faced in making *Star Wars* was made just that little bit easier by conceptual artist Ralph McQuarrie, whose art was instrumental in demonstrating Lucas's not-always-easy-to-envision dream of what *Star Wars* should look like.

Star Wars would probably still have been made without Ralph McQuarrie's input, but it would have been very different, and possibly less successful, had he not been one of the first people hired by George Lucas and his producer, Gary Kurtz, on the original *Star Wars*.

George Lucas said it best when he remarked, "When words could not convey my ideas, I could always point to one of Ralph's fabulous illustrations and say, 'Do it like this.'"

Sadly, McQuarrie passed away in 2012, but his amazing art lives on, a constant source of inspiration to the makers of the new *Star Wars* movies and, most obviously, to the team behind *Star Wars Rebels*.

Since his death, his friends, Paul Bateman and Stan Stice, whose encyclopedic knowledge of Ralph's work has been of great use in the making of *Star Wars Insider* on numerous occasions, have become great friends and collaborators on the magazine. These guys are the keepers of an amazing legacy, and there can be no better protectors as McQuarrie's art continues to be the key building block with which all *Star Wars* is made.
—**Jonathan Wilkins**

*Born **Ralph Angus McQuarrie** on June 13, 1929, in Gary, Indiana, McQuarrie served in the United States Army during the Korean War. In the 1960s, he moved to California on his return from Korea, studying at the Art Center School in downtown Los Angeles. Initially he worked for a dentistry firm, providing illustrations of teeth and dental equipment, before he was hired as an illustrator at Boeing. He also designed film posters, and provided animation for CBS News's coverage of the Apollo space program for Reel Three. It was there that he was asked by Hal Barwood to produce illustrations for a film project he and Matthew Robbins were starting. His work soon caught the eye of George Lucas, who enlisted him to help envisage what was then entitled, The Star Wars....*

GRAND DESIGNS

INDUSTRIAL LIGHT & MAGIC
The Art of Special Effects

THOMAS G. SMITH

Above: The battle over the surface of the Death Star: a production painting from the original *Star Wars*.

Right: Ralph McQuarrie at his desk—inside the art department at Elstree Studios during the making of *The Empire Strikes Back.*

IN 1984, WHEN ILM GENERAL MANAGER, THOMAS G. SMITH, WAS RESEARCHING AND WRITING *INDUSTRIAL LIGHT & MAGIC: THE ART OF SPECIAL EFFECTS*, HE INTERVIEWED SEVERAL KEY ILM-ERS, INCLUDING RALPH MCQUARRIE, WHO PASSED AWAY ON MARCH 3, 2012. SMITH HAS GENEROUSLY GIVEN THESE DECADES-OLD TAPES TO *INSIDER*, AS ONLY A FRACTION OF THEIR CONTENT MADE IT INTO THE ORIGINAL BOOK. INTERVIEW BY THOMAS G. SMITH

Star Wars Insider: How did you originally come to be interested in art?

Ralph McQuarrie: I started looking at paintings when I was a kid. My mother and grandfather painted and drew. My grandfather had this little publication he did and he was an important man in my hometown in Montana. I was interested in going to art class before the age of 10. There was an art class at the polytechnic school (a school for teachers) in Billings. People would supervise classes of little kids to learn how to teach. I wasn't able to do that, but I was able to major in art before

I left high school. I had pretty well settled on the idea of being a commercial artist before I left. I started working as a technical illustrator after a few months of instruction on isometric drawing at the YMCA technical school that was set up after World War II.

In 1949, I went into this school for technical illustrators and the instructor liked my drawings. I was doing quite a lot of drawings for myself and he suggested I become a painter. I hadn't had many art lessons, but I'd read books on painters and art, and I had a pretty good art-school teacher in high school talk to me quite a bit about the possibilities.

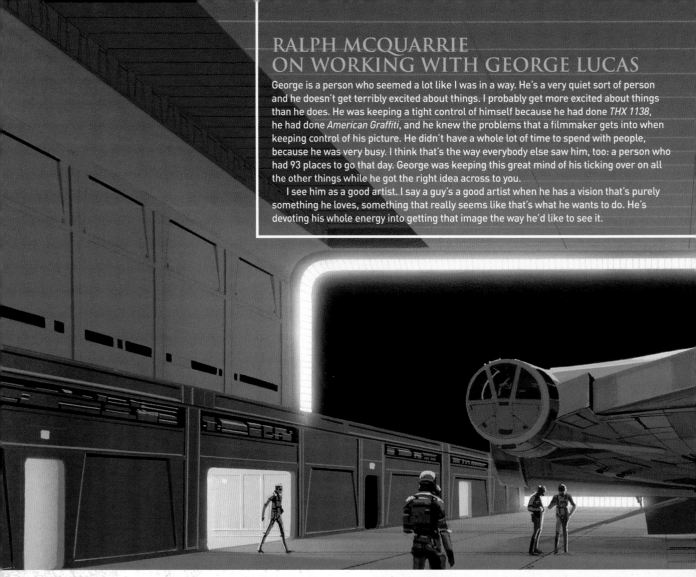

RALPH MCQUARRIE
ON WORKING WITH GEORGE LUCAS

George is a person who seemed a lot like I was in a way. He's a very quiet sort of person and he doesn't get terribly excited about things. I probably get more excited about things than he does. He was keeping a tight control of himself because he had done *THX 1138*, he had done *American Graffiti*, and he knew the problems that a filmmaker gets into when keeping control of his picture. He didn't have a whole lot of time to spend with people, because he was very busy. I think that's the way everybody else saw him, too: a person who had 93 places to go that day. George was keeping this great mind of his ticking over on all the other things while he got the right idea across to you.

I see him as a good artist. I say a guy's a good artist when he has a vision that's purely something he loves, something that really seems like that's what he wants to do. He's devoting his whole energy into getting that image the way he'd like to see it.

Above:
The *Millennium Falcon* onboard the Death Star.

Above, right:
Legendary CBS anchorman, Walter Cronkite, visits ILM, speaking with McQuarrie as George Lucas looks on.

Right:
Ralph at work at Elstree.

Far right:
The core team of the *Empire* matte painting department: Harrison Ellenshaw (sitting); standing, from left to right: Michael Pangrazio, Craig Barron, McQuarrie, and Neil Krepela.

I got a job at the Boeing Company in Seattle and started working as a technical illustrator. I was the youngest technical illustrator in the group of about 50 or so and we did repair manuals and parts catalogues. I worked there until sometime in 1950 when I was drafted and went into the Army during the Korean War. I spent two years in the Army—11 months of that was in Korea.

That must have been a pretty miserable place to be.
I thought I was never going to get out of there alive. I got in so many close shaves. There were skirmishes, combat patrols, and a continual exchange of artillery and mortars. There were some fairly major actions that I was involved in, around about the end of the time that I was there, which resulted in a lot of casualties, including myself.

I got hit square up the side of the head with a round from a Russian "Burp Gun." If it had been an automatic, it would've killed me for sure because they spray out about 500 rounds a minute.

Luckily, it hit my helmet and became caught up in the webbing. It slammed into

my head, went through the helmet, the steel, and pierced the liner.

I thought a grenade had gone off close to us, because I'd just seen a grenade rolling down the side of a hill. We were standing in a trench and the Chinese were on the other side of this hill, which was about 13 yards away. They were throwing grenades at us and we were throwing grenades at them. I was still standing there with this hand grenade; luckily, I hadn't pulled the pin.

I wouldn't have known exactly what happened to me but for the fact that my helmet had a bullet hole in it. The medics didn't believe me. They didn't really believe what had happened: They looked at the side of my head and said, "Well, it could use a couple of stitches," and sent me back to hospital for a few days.

> ## "GEORGE LUCAS IS A PERSON WHO SEEMED A LOT LIKE I WAS IN A WAY."

It must have had a terrifying after-effect, too?
I heard later that a lot of people came back and said that they were embarrassed to be alive and that they felt very ashamed to be a survivor when so many people died that they knew well. That's the way I felt. I think underneath it was kind of subliminal. Coming back to my job was very hard for me and I just felt vaguely disturbed, for a long time. It made a lot of difference to my life, that's very true.

How did you first get approached to work on *Star Wars*?
I first met George Lucas in 1973 through producers Hal Barwood and Matthew Robbins. They had a script they wanted to make into a film [*Star Dancing*] and they hadn't done anything with it yet. Their agent thought that an illustration would be good. They had seen some of my work and they knew a guy that I worked with at a place where we were doing stuff for the Apollo missions. So, through them, I met George one day—this was just about the time he was finishing *American Graffiti*. George saw my slides and we talked about *Star Wars*, even though it didn't even have a title yet.

George remembered me when he got around to approaching Fox. I think the ideas he had were very much from an illustrator's point of view. In other

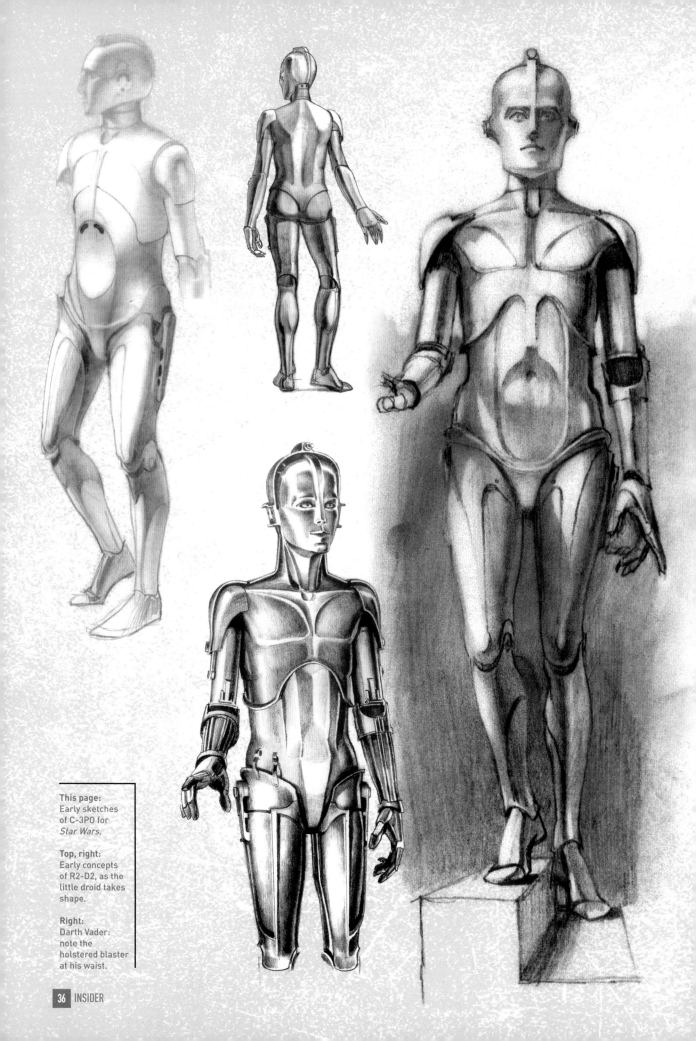

This page:
Early sketches
of C-3PO for
Star Wars.

Top, right:
Early concepts
of R2-D2, as the
little droid takes
shape.

Right:
Darth Vader:
note the
holstered blaster
at his waist.

words, the whole film was kind of motivated by this desire to see these things on the screen.

George and Gary Kurtz stopped by with a script. George had his second draft and left it with me. We sort of arranged right there in that 20-minute meeting what I was going to do. They wanted four or five paintings to take into Fox. So they said, "Just read it, find some things that you think are good to illustrate." So I had sketches and things for him the first time he came back. I had sketches of Artoo-Detoo and had started thinking about Darth Vader and See-Threepio.

Had you done much film work before you started working with George?
Nothing but animated films, and I'd done some storyboards for Encyclopedia Britannica. I worked with John Carlo-Louis on a film called *Time*.

I was there that day when George showed *THX 1138.4EB*, his student film, at Britannica. I thought it was really great. I was amazed at how good it was.

Did the script describe the droids or was their look something you came up with?
I think Artoo was just described as a small robot. I thought of him as running on a giant ball bearing —just a sphere, a circle, wheel-like. He had gyros so he could go in any direction on this ball. Gary and George visited England to see about studios and craftsmen and so forth, and I continued to work on more paintings. Then, one day, George finally came back in and said, 'Well, looks like this is 'go.'"

Did George just give you the material to read and you did the paintings?

We had quite a few exchanges because I had strong feelings about it. There were things like Darth Vader's mask, which evolved from concerns I had about him dying on the way between the two spaceships [in the second draft, Vader descends through space to attack the Rebel ship]. I thought he ought to have some sort of breathing apparatus or he's going to die out there! George looked, and I don't think it was the kind of thing that really bothered him, but he said, "Well, give him some sort of breath mask." So I started designing breath masks, and in the interim designed the general look for Darth Vader. George okayed that, and I don't think he thought we would keep the mask on him all through the picture. In the end, it was logical for him to keep the mask on for the wholepicture. Why take it off? There could be a mysterious reason for him having to wear it, which nobody needed to know about.

Did you also have a hand in designing the costumes for Han Solo, Princess Leia, and Luke?
I did sketches just to illustrate the central idea. The general look and "leg wrapping" thing for Luke came from a sketch I had done. I should've got some credit for the costumes because I designed most of them, in essence, with John Mollo and his crew making changes to some of them.

The Stormtroopers were definitely mine. I made the biggest contribution

"GEORGE SAID, 'GIVE VADER SOME KIND OF BREATH MASK!'"

from a design point of view, simply because—at first—I was the only designer working on it. If John Barry had come in earlier, I'm sure a lot more of it would've been his. I think John liked what I'd done, and with his theatrical sense of good drama—of how to put things together, how to move the camera through things and how to get a good foreground going—he took

elements that I had used and just kind of enlarged them to become more suitable sets. His touch was very, very important in how the film worked. It certainly made the film what it was. Although he used my work kind of like reference material, he was able to draw from it, with his own bolder sense.

Main image: Stormtroopers corner the Rebels on the Death Star.

Right: The troops patrol production designer, John Barry's Death Star corridors, a result of his collaboration with McQuarrie.

Above, far right: An early take on Han and Chewie!

Above, right: An early variation on the Stormtrooper helmet.

Below, right: Ralph's stunning matte painting of the *Millennium Falcon* at **Cloud City** for *The Empire Strikes Back.*

THE ART OF MATTE PAINTING

Ralph McQuarrie on the secret art. My spaceships weren't really that good; I tended to get a little old-fashioned-looking with them. They weren't quite zippy enough for John Dykstra. George Lucas said, 'Well, work on the matte paintings' with Harrison Ellenshaw. So, I went up to Disney one day and looked at the matte paintings. I'd never seen any before. I looked at them and thought *Gee, they look awfully painterly to me. I don't see how these work on the screen.* I had to think through the process—how do you blow a painting up on the big screen and make it work? I found out the screen wasn't all that big. It's a big screen from where you're sitting, but when you hold your arms up sight-size, it's fairly small and hardly occupies your peripheral vision.

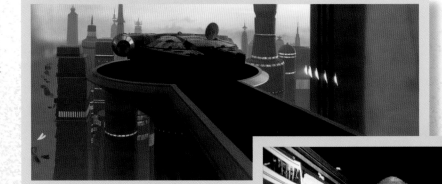

I realized if you made a painting three or four feet wide, it was going to get reduced in a sense. It was also going to be broken up into the grain of the film so that all the little brushstrokes and the

edges and so forth are softened. I think that's the reason that the paintings work on the screen.

Harrison said, "If you put a lot of detail in and are very careful that every little thing reads like an illustration, it looks like an illustration on the screen." You've got to obscure things a bit in such a way that your vision blurs things together. Of course, most of the paintings deal with the background, which is very frequently low on focus anyway, so things are on the soft side and a little obscured.

What was the process for this?
Harrison would put the clip in the camera at ILM and I would trace out the drawing on tissue. Most of the paintings that I did were just items that floated; like planets or the Death Star, which didn't particularly have any foreground elements. [For *Empire*], if they were going to add things that moved, like foreground figures that were done against a bluescreen, I'd just

"YOU'VE GOT TO OBSCURE THINGS SO YOUR VISION BLURS THINGS TOGETHER."

lay it out so that I knew I had a diagram to show the camera crew where to put the figures.

So, you didn't have to actually color-match anything?
No, it was just a matter of a gray wall. Everything else in the Death Star was gray. You'd maybe put a little color into the gray, maybe a little warm gray or cool gray.

I did quite a few paintings that I don't think got used. I made a matte painting that was a total sphere, which looked fine as a still, but it didn't look good when the camera moved in on it—the perspective wouldn't change on the screen so it looked kind of flat when it moved. I made a lot of paintings of the surface that I thought could be used to track in on, but they didn't do that. They used some of them; they looked pretty good.

Did you do some of those paintings of the reactor chamber when Obi-Wan is sneaking around?
Yeah, there was one painting looking down to show the tremendous height—that's one Harrison did. I did several showing similar things in tunnels and corridors that had plunging walls, and I completed them onto the studio floor there and I just carried the painting on down to show how far this wall went down.

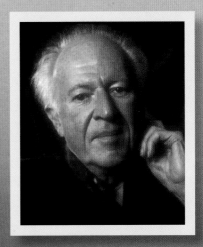

Did you do other film work in the gap between *Star Wars* **and** *The Empire Strikes Back*?
I did some work on *Star Trek: The Motion Picture* with [production designer] Ken Adam, on a version that didn't get made [*Star Trek: Planet of the Titans*]. I worked on *Battlestar Galactica* for a while, too. Then we got into preliminary design on *The Empire Strikes Back*.

I went to England for six months [during principal photography]. It was interesting for me to be there and see what went on. When I got back, I had given up my apartment in L.A., so I had to send my stuff to ILM to where it was stored. I came back to do matte paintings for *Empire*.

How do you judge a painting to be finished?
I did two or three sketches for Artoo-Detoo [for the first film] and said, "Gee, that's interesting, but I don't know why I think that's good." I just put it aside. Basically, my thinking was that what I was doing wasn't final; somebody else was going to come along and design this stuff.

I did a couple of sketches of the Tusken Raiders. George had said they were a nomadic kind of mutated creatures that lived in the desert. I wrapped their faces up, because I thought of the area and sandstorms and that kind of thing. I also thought of them as being perhaps mutants with kind of tender flesh, they were sort of on the verge of barely surviving, so they had masks and goggles as protection. In the third or fourth sketch, I thought, *That looks right. I put it aside and went on to something else.*

I look back at the art that I did on *Star Wars* and think, *They were really the best.* I was having a good time and I didn't think my art would ever be published.

Were you involved in the early design work on *The Empire Strikes Back*?
Yes, I was involved with Joe Johnston in Los Angeles. We worked at home, the same as we did on *Star Wars*. I would work at home and bring my drawings in. I'd call up, or they would call me and say George was coming in and would you like to come by with your stuff to show him.

George had an office at Universal and we met there every week or so. They just had a small space, but it had a Xerox machine. I suppose they established that office during *American Graffiti*.

You worked with matte artist Michael Pangrazio on *The Empire Strikes Back*.
He showed a lot of energy, enthusiasm, and confidence. He came back and watched me paint for a little while. Prior to that time, he had done everything with airbrush. He would do great big things; all kinds of careful work. He could paint better than I could—and before I turned around, practically! He worked on *Empire* as a kind of matte painting helper. His potential emerged as soon as he started to paint. He painted all those big backdrops first [for Hoth], and it looked terrific. He tackled the things with oil paints and it looked great, right from the first painting. I did one with this old spray brush and I used acrylics. I had a lot of time with it and it looked pretty good. Mike looked at it, immediately saw

Main image: A probe droid patrols the icy plains of Hoth in McQuarrie's production illustration.
Above: Ralph McQuarrie.

Main image: McQuarrie's stunning painting of Cloud City.

Opposite page, from top: Approaching Cloud City—a view from inside; the cloud cars observe flying whales above Cloud City. While these creatures were never realized for *The Empire Strikes Back*, they did eventually show up in *Attack of Clones*.

what was wrong with it, and they fiddled around and used part of it for one shot.

What was the shot?
It's the first shot you see of the Imperial Walkers coming toward you, and it had kind of a hazy background. It looked fine on the screen really. Mike was very particular and meticulous about things and I think the painting would've looked good the way I envisioned it, but it didn't matter; it looked good the way he suggested it was shot. He went on to do the rest of the paintings and I thought they looked gorgeous, just loaded with finesse and a strong sensibility of what had to be done with the paintings.

How about Joe Johnston? You worked more with him than these others.
Joe was just a young person out of school. He had the sort of industrial designer background that suited him ideally for what he did there with the spacecraft on *Star Wars*. His drawings of the Death Star, I thought, were very, very impressive. He really had a lot of imagination and a fine touch. He was a really good draughtsman. As I watched him progress through *Empire* and *Jedi*, his drawings became more sophisticated, and so did his sense of what was needed in

the way of drama. He invented quite a few things that made the story work. George just threw sequences at him, like the battle in the forest with the Ewoks and the space battles. Joe seemed to pull those together with his own sense of what an exciting flow of film was going to bring to the audience. He invented a lot of stuff and added humor, and that can make a scene work.

They say that there are some people who are keen on holographic thinking: In other words, they have a good three-dimensional concept of everything. I'm certain that Joe is in that category, as am I. I'm not good on linear thinking at all: I don't put sentences together particularly well, or remember numbers, and I cannot do mathematics worth a dime. I'm pretty good at physics, though. I was given problems there that dealt with three-dimensional things. I suppose I could've been an engineer. I was very interested in engineering and aircraft and I still love to fool around with models and so forth. But it's that holographic-thinking side of the brain

"MY MIND JUST TAKES OVER AND MAKES UP IMAGES FOR EVERYTHING."

that makes a person who's potentially going to be a mechanical engineer or an artist.

What type of critiques did George Lucas give you?
Well, on most things, especially on *Star Wars*, he had his script pretty well full of descriptive passages, which were good. I like to read scripts and I like to read books—my mind just takes over and makes up images for everything. When I'm reading I'm going through the whole place that this thing is happening in, and in time with what's going on. When I was working on my sketches I would have the sound in mind and the motion of the camera because that's the way I read. If I'm listening to music when I'm going through some place, if I'm really into it, listening to it, I'm there in some kind of environment having this kind of a dream and that's what I'm doing when I'm working on these films.

How was George to work with?
I can't see where George has had

THE POWER OF PERSEVERANCE

"I had to work hard for years to get to a position where I could learn to make things look pretty good. I kind of shied away from it for a long time. I got sort of burned in my early experiences. I went back to technical illustrating; I gave up the idea of being an editorial illustrator. I never thought I'd ever be a film designer. It wasn't something that had occurred to me."

"*E.T.: The Extra-Terrestrial* was pretzell scripted when I first talked to Steven Spielberg about it. He was interested in my ideas on the promotion of the film. Steven had decided I should be in on making the poster. He had me doing poster ideas at first, then he said that he needed a spaceship. He said that it should be a kind of goofy-looking ship that looked like maybe it was made by Dr. Seuss. I sat and drew seven or eight spaceships one day, thinking about what Dr. Seuss would do, only not really knowing! I included things that kind of hung out, little spindly things and that sort of stuff. I thought the one with the spherical form would be the best and Steven liked that, too. He even liked my ideas about the sound of its engines—I said on my little sketch that it might have the sound of a 747, that whine with a whisper and the thunder of the exhaust. It would be some other, magical quality that gave it the thrust, a sort of mad gravity. It was very quick, like the spaceship I did for *Close Encounters*. I worked a couple of days on *E.T.* in total."

any spare time in the last eight or nine years. He's always been on a film. He goes to bed with the problems of the film on his mind and I guess he wakes up and they're still with him. It's just a mad whirlwind of activity, and every little thing amounts to $50,000 dollars here, $80,000 there and everything he says costs money or saves money or time, and time is money. It's very important to be on the ball.

I felt all the time I worked for him that I was a filmmaker's helper and whatever I could do to contribute to the film, I would throw it in. I knew it was his film and that his decisions were my decisions in a way. He would talk to me about what he needed from everyone else and through his script and through his words, which were very sparing. I appreciated that, because it gives you some latitude to work. If somebody has described every little thing, it gets awkward. George is very good at giving little guiding pushes, a little something to bounce off of. He liked to see a lot of sketches and then something would turn up in the course of doing them.

He said to me on a number of occasions that he was surprised about how easily we arrived at things sometimes and then we would go straight onto the next thing. ☺

Main image: The attack on the Death Star II, an image from the McQuarrie portfolio.

From above: A tauntaun ends up as a wampa's lunch. (*The Illustrated Star Wars Universe*)

Below, left: A portfolio piece showing the wildlife on Dagobah. **Below:** A production illustration showing another fearsome beast!

"I like Norman Rockwell's
illustrations very much.
I just think they're wonderful.
I used to love the illustrator
Robert Fawcett. He was
an illustrator in the 1950s
who drew beautiful, elegant
drawings. I also liked René
Magritte, who did surrealistic
art. There's not really a
drawing that I don't find
interesting. There's something
there, you can see it in all
the little ways people handle
things. I like Maxfield Parish,
N.C. Wyeth, and Andrew Wyeth,
too. I like the figurative artists
best. I like to see a painting
that looks like something."

RALPH ON ART

"To me, painting is a very slight thing, music
is a much more important art. It's the art that
comes into your body and takes over your bones
and thumps on your chest. I think it's really what
generates emotion. If you listen to film music,
which is very much designed to get an emotional
response out of people, you'll find out how music
serves to stimulate you emotionally and it does
it very well. Paintings do a certain amount, but
until your eye is wandering over a thing and it's
in three dimensions, it doesn't quite have the
same impact."

STAR WARS
INSIDER

ISSUE 136
October 2012
U.S. $7.99
CAN $9.99

TITAN

7 25274 22493 7

CARRIE FISHER
PRINCESS LEIA ORGANA

ISSUE 136
OCTOBER 2012

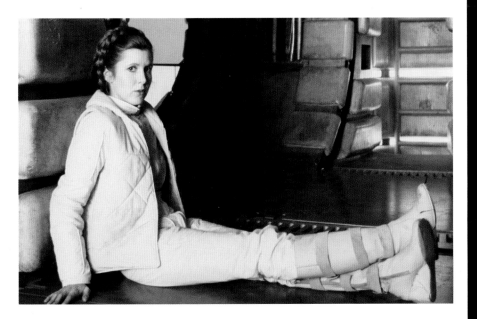

Beautiful, feisty and charming, Princess Leia is much like Carrie Fisher herself. Candid and indiscreet, you never quite know what you're going to get with Carrie.

This interview came courtesy of Lucasfilm's J. W. Rinzler, who supplied *Insider* with this, along with the Mark Hamill and Harrison Ford interviews that feature elsewhere in the book. This, as far as I am aware, is the first *Star Wars*-related interview Fisher ever gave, so is of great historical interest. It's fascinating as it paints a picture of Fisher at that time. Despite their wildly different backgrounds, she, like Hamill, talks about reading comic books and her love of watching old movies. Unlike her co-star, she came from a radically different background, being the daughter of two iconic Hollywood stars.

She's always a popular, and unpredictable, guest on the convention circuit where she is usually accompanied by her dog, Gary.—**Jonathan Wilkins**

Carrie Frances Fisher was born on October 21, 1956. The daughter of Hollywood royalty, her parents are actress Debbie Reynolds and singer, Eddie Fisher. Fisher made her movie debut in the 1975 movie Shampoo, *alongside Warren Beatty and Julie Christie. This was followed by a diverse series of roles, including work with Woody Allen, Rob Reiner, Sidney Lumet, and David Cronenberg. An accomplished writer, her bestselling novel* Postcards from the Edge *was also the screenplay for the film of the same name, as well as her autobiographical one-woman play and the non-fiction book,* Wishful Drinking *based on the show. Fisher has also enjoyed a successful career as a leading script doctor, including work on* Hook, Lethal Weapon 3, Sister Act, Mr. and Mrs. Smith, *and all of the* Star Wars *prequels.*

KEEP CALM AND CARRIE ON!

BEFORE *STAR WARS* FIRST HIT THE THEATERS, CHARLES LIPPINCOTT, LUCASFILM VICE PRESIDENT OF MARKETING AND MERCHANDISING, TALKED WITH MANY OF THE KEY CAST AND CREW ON THE MAKING OF THE FILM. WHEN LIPPINCOTT SPOKE WITH CARRIE FISHER ON JANUARY 4, 1977, THEY DISCUSSED THE YOUNG STAR'S INTERESTS IN OLD FILMS, COMIC BOOKS, AND LITERATURE, ABOUT BECOMING AN ACTRESS—AND ON BEING SILLY.

WHETHER LEADING AN ESCAPE FROM THE DEATH STAR OR BIDING HER TIME CHAINED TO JABBA THE HUTT, PRINCESS LEIA ALWAYS MANAGES TO LOOK HER REGAL BEST.

1 Diplomatic mission outfit (*A New Hope*) The perfect look for a princess, although less practical for running around the Death Star. Her astonishing "cinnamon buns" hairstyle is easily cinema's most iconic, "do."

2 Ewok style! (*Return of the Jedi*) Leia is clearly the kind of girl who looks good no matter what. When she arrives unexpectedly in the village of a primitive tribe, the Ewoks just happen to have an outfit in her size. Either that or there's an Ewok tailor skilled at making clothes fit for a woodland princess.

Charles Lippincott: When did you decide you wanted to get into entertainment? **Carrie Fisher:** I don't remember, but it was always assumed that I would do it, so I kind of went along with that assumption.

For a very short time, I did want to be a teacher. One of my teachers had her room all pink, even pink chalk, and I thought that was really neat. She had committed herself to making the room pink and it seemed like she had a lot of power, and I kind of wanted that power that she had. I also wanted to be a stewardess, so I could travel; I don't know why, because I hate planes—although I can't hate them too much because I fly around a lot. But mostly, I always wanted to do this, acting.

Was acting just something you were drawn into?
When I was in 6th grade, I did my first play. I played a squaw in the 7th grade production—it was really big stuff! I was the big kid on campus that year. And I used to take musical comedy courses. I always liked it; it was like recess to me. And it was a way of getting out of school, too.

You didn't like school?
No, I don't think so. Some of it I liked. I hated math, like the rest of the kids. Math and liver, just like everybody else! I don't remember ever thinking, *I think I'll go into show-business*.

You know, Halloween was ridiculous at our house—and you get an endless Halloween when you're an actress. You get to dress up and pretend you're somebody else, all the time. I like doing that.

You started out singing. When did you start acting? Or was it always a combination of both?
I think it was always a combination of both. I wanted to do musicals, early on. But the singing stuff started first.

Stage musicals or movie musicals?
Both. They don't do them anymore, all that Judy Garland stuff.

This is all a form of fantasy.
Musicals are. Because you have to be willing to be fools just like in fantasy stuff. But now they're getting more realistic.

Then there is a realistic fantasy, like *Taxi Driver*... which pretends to be realism, but is really fantasy. It's borderline, almost schizophrenic.
It uses that one element where it exceeds reality. But when I saw *2001*, I liked pretending that I understood that movie. I was really young when I saw that. We saw it a couple of times.

I hear you're interested in certain types of singers, big band singers like Helen Forrest?
My mother [actress Debbie Reynolds] had a nightclub act on the road when I was 13, and I started listening to everything. I loved old songs and I loved old movies. Helen Forrest sang "Skylark," I think. I love big bands and I used to go to Vegas—at about three—not a great place for a kid, but I would go there and it was just more than you could know what to do with. There was this huge band and I was overwhelmed.

"OUR HOUSE WAS ON THE STAR MAP, SO PEOPLE WOULD COME BY AND TAKE PICTURES ALL THE TIME."

Previous spread: Carrie Fisher poses for a PR still (not her favorite pastime) during production on *A New Hope*.

Top left: Leia takes command in the Rebel war room on Yavin IV.

Left, opposite page: Pret-a-Logray? Fashion by the Ewoks!

This page: Leia, princess with an attitude!

Top right: Calling the shots on Cloud City as Billy Dee Williams (Lando) looks on.

Who did you hang out with as a kid?

Kids my own age, my brother, for a time. We used to put on skits and we always played something or other. When I grew up, there were always cameras around. If something was going on, my mother would say, "Wait, let me get the camera." So we were always doing stuff in front of the camera.

And also, our house was on the movie star map, so people would drive by and take pictures of us all of the time. So I have this thing about that—I don't like having stills taken of me at all. I start to get crazy and I sweat. I never sweat—hey, I'm like a Barbie doll! But I don't like stills much, because I can never pretend the camera isn't there. But I always liked the movie camera, because you could always do what you wanted and you didn't have to worry about standing a certain way or being still. And we used to make home movies all the time.

We got started on movies really early because we had a projection room. We were privileged: We used to always get movies at the house. There was a book of all the movies you could rent, and we would just go crazy. That was fun.

Those years were very movie-orientated. That's how I grew up, so I don't know anything about anything else. I can't do anything else. I can't! Don't make me!

What about reading? Were you ever into fantasy books?

I used to read books before I could read. I used to look at them and make up stories to go along with them. I used to go in the closet and read books. I'd go in with my flashlight and read books aloud to myself. There are a lot of good kids' books. *The Secret Garden* is good.

I did a lot of reading when I was a kid. That's why no one was really worried when I dropped out of high school—except me, now...!

So what were your interests in reading?

When I went to Central [a drama school in London], they gave you a lot of classics to read, which I hadn't really read. And Shakespeare. But before that, everything: Hemingway, Fitzgerald, and so forth. I wanted to do all of that. There was a group of us that would go through one author at a time.

What age was this?

About 14 or 15. We also read George Orwell (*1984* and *Animal Farm*). Orwell is sort of science fiction, isn't it?

Do you like sci-fi books and movies?

When I was about 14, I saw a movie on television that scared the hell

3 Sultry Slave (*Return of the Jedi*)

She may look beautiful, but she's not helpless, as Jabba would later learn the hard way. Leia's gold bikini may be worn grudgingly, but male fans will be thinking of Han's line from a deleted scene from *Empire*: "You should wear girls' clothes all the time."

out of me. I don't even know what it was, but it took place on the moon. I used to be afraid of Martians coming down. There was an invisible Martian in the movie. He had an electric field about 10 feet high and if you got thrown into that—ARGGHH!—you died. That riveted me, so I went out and got some science fiction.

I've heard you like Ray Bradbury. Do you like his strong style of writing or the stories?

Both. He isn't even one of the most well-known scientists among people who don't know that much about science fiction. He's one of the most read.

Lately, I've seen a lot of science fiction films. There was one they showed on television where the Gods give one man power—*The Man Who Could Work Miracles*. And then there are ones with Raymond Massey in *Things to Come* and *Transatlantic Tunnel*.

Really? You saw those in London or here?

New York. They have festivals all the time on certain types of films.

Did you ever read comics?

Yeah. *Archie* for a brief period. Then my favorites were those *Love* comics. They still have them and I am still riveted by them. They give you dating tips, which are my favorite! How to say no, how to act if you want to get kissed goodnight. They have *True Love*, and *Young Romance* and *Just Married*. That's one of my favorites. I read one

where a couple got married and on the honeymoon the bride realized it was just a crush. They were some of the most bizarre stories you ever read in your life, and I love those.

There are a series of terrible comic books out. One called *Slime*, one called *Despair*. The covers are really funny. I don't really read them. I just like the covers.

Do you ever watch much TV?
Some. The terrible kind. I used to deliberately fake being sick so I could stay home and watch *Andy of Mayberry*. There were four shows—one right after the other in the morning—that I used to love to watch. I like *I Love Lucy* a lot. *The Real McCoys*. *Outer Limits*! I did watch that. The one guy went up to Mars and came back with a terrible disease. And also came back with plants that bled and were alive and would kill people.... All that stuff was fun. Bleeding plants, it's great.

I used to watch the old movies, like a Loretta Young movie and stuff like that.

Which other old movies?
Everything. Comedies. I used to go through the *TV Guide* and check off the comedies and make sure I'd be home for that. Cary Grant and Irene Dunne, Frank Capra. The sophisticated ones.

You aren't interested in Laurel and Hardy?
Oh! Riveted. Moved. Destroyed by them. Oh, yes. I bought a *TV Guide* and made sure I saw every movie in it. *Way Out West*. Every one of them. Oh, I loved them.... And the Marx

Above: Working with Peter Cushing (far left) and George Lucas (middle) on *A New Hope*.

This page: Ready to repel the forces of evil in *The Empire Strikes Back*.

LEIA'S GREATEST LOOKS!

4 Braided for battle (*The Empire Strikes Back*)
Leia's braided hair and no-nonsense military attire on Hoth show she means business, whether defending the rebel base or herself from Han Solo's amorous advances!

5 Cloud City (*The Empire Strikes Back*)
Lando said it best: "You look absolutely beautiful. You truly belong with us here in the clouds." The old smoothie!

Brothers in *Night at the Opera*. We used to watch that all the time. We had a copy of that once and got a projector and ran it about six times. We watched some of it backward.... The scene with all of the people going into the state room, and then the door opens and all of the people pour out. Most comedies, I love them. Then I started liking the real movies.

We used to go out to Westwood and go from one theater to the other and live for when the movie was going to come out. That's what people mostly talked about. We would mostly talk about when movies were coming out. That's all I ever did when I was a kid.

> "WHEN I WAS 16, MY MOTHER DID A HORROR MOVIE AND SHE DIED IN IT. I'M GLAD SHE DIDN'T DO IT WHEN I WAS YOUNGER."

Did you like *Ryan's Daughter*?
We'd go to see *Gone with the Wind* and all of those... And I always wanted to know how they did all of the effects in there because I was real scared. There were the scenes with blood.

When I was 16, my mother did a horror movie and she died in it. *What's the Matter with Helen*. In the last shot, she was dead with blood running out of her mouth. I'm glad she didn't do it when I was younger. She said she waited. But I always wanted to know how that was done. I would sometimes watch her film, but not that much. One time, when I was really young, I saw her in old woman make-up, in *How the West Was Won*. She got dressed up to look about 50, and it was amazing. It was magic. I couldn't figure out how they'd done it and I always wanted to do that. I like knowing how they do the tricks.

Did she take you on set often?
When she'd go on location, we used to go and visit her. It looked fun. It looked like everyone was having a good time. They probably weren't.... But when I was a kid it looked like grown-up recess. ♛

"CHARMING, TO THE LAST."

CLASSIC PUT-DOWNS FROM THE PRINCESS OF PITH!

"Will someone get this walking carpet out of my way?"
Ouch! What did Chewie do to deserve that? (*ANH*)

"Would it help if I got out and pushed?"
Careful what you say to the designated driver, your highness! (*ESB*)

"Darth Vader. Only you could be so bold."
A teenager is sarcastic to her parent—with a twist!! (*ANH*)

"Governor Tarkin, I should have expected to find you holding Vader's leash. I recognized your foul stench when I was brought on board."
Not only was Tarkin evil, but he also had personal hygiene issues! (*ANH*)

"You're a jittery little thing, aren't you?"
Careful, Leia—he looks cute but he's also carrying a very sharp spear! (*ROTJ*)

"I don't know where you get your delusions, laser brain!"
Arguing with Han—Leia in denial! (*ESB*)

STAR WARS

INSIDER

ISSUE 145
NOV/DEC 2013
U.S. $7.99
Can $9.99

TITAN

GEORGE LUCAS
CREATOR OF *STAR WARS* AND
ALAN DEAN FOSTER
AUTHOR OF *SPLINTER OF THE MIND'S EYE*

ISSUE 145
NOVEMBER/DECEMBER 2013

What is there to say about the man who started the whole phenomenon? A true success story of the little guy taking on the system, it seems strange that a biopic hasn't yet been produced. *Star Wars* was always a triumph of George Lucas's imagination. The story of its making is familiar to those with even the most casual interest in the saga featuring assorted difficulties and hindrances challenging even Lucas's indomitable tenacity. For a film subtitled *A New Hope*, hope seemed in pretty short supply during *Star Wars'* fraught production period.

This transcript was first mentioned to me by J. W. Rinzler for inclusion in *Star Wars Insider* back in 2007. It seemed too good to be true. As a boy, I'd loved *Splinter of the Mind's Eye,* with its evocative and mysterious Ralph McQuarrie cover and its back cover promising a confrontation involving Darth Vader, mysterious crystals, and a fight for life on an inhospitable jungle planet.

What I hadn't realized was that the book had a wildly intriguing history. Written by Alan Dean Foster, who had authored the novelization of *Star Wars*, the book was supervised by Lucas, who felt that if a cheap sequel was required, this would be an acceptable low-budget template.

The piece that follows offers a real insight into how burned-out Lucas was by the trauma of making the first film. With his labor of love in post-production, the future of *Star Wars* was hanging precariously in the balance....
—Jonathan Wilkins

George Walton Lucas, Jr., (born May 14, 1944), was raised in Modesto, California, the son of Dorothy Ellinore Lucas and George Walton Lucas, Sr., who owned and ran a stationery store.

Growing up, Lucas had a passion for cars and motor racing. Dreaming of becoming a race-car driver, he spent most of his high school years racing on the underground circuit at fairgrounds and hanging out at garages. On June 12, 1962, while driving his souped-up Autobianchi Bianchina, he crashed and was very nearly killed. While this dampened his dream of being a professional driver, he would always be interested in motorsports, and attends events even to this day.

Following the crash, he enrolled at Modesto Junior College, where he studied anthropology, sociology, and literature, amongst other subjects. He began using an 8mm camera to film car races, which inspired his early short film, 1:42.08 at the University of Southern California, where he enrolled in its School of Cinema, and later formed the backdrop of what would be his breakthrough film, American Graffiti.

Alan Dean Foster was born November 18, 1946. An American writer of fantasy and science fiction, Foster has written numerous standalone novels, but is best-known for his novelizations of film scripts, writing adaptations of big franchise titles such as Alien, Star Trek, Transformers, *and* The Terminator.

THE CONVERSATION

GEORGE LUCAS AND ALAN DEAN FOSTER DISCUSS THE STORY OF WHAT WOULD BECOME *SPLINTER OF THE MIND'S EYE*—AND THUS REVEAL A FASCINATING GLIMPSE INTO LUCAS'S CREATIVE MIND MANY MONTHS BEFORE THE HUGE SUCCESS OF *STAR WARS* WOULD CHANGE THE WORLD! WORDS: J. W. RINZLER

Attendees: GEORGE LUCAS, ALAN DEAN FOSTER, and Lucasfilm vice president of marketing and merchandising CHARLES LIPPINCOTT

On October 13, 1976, George Lucas sat down with Alan Dean Foster to discuss Foster's second *Star Wars* book. Foster had already ghostwritten the *Star Wars* novelization, which was to be published later that year under George Lucas's name. At the time of their conversation, Lucas was still recovering from his difficult shoot in Tunisia and England—and from the horror of discovering, upon his return, that his effects facility had made very little progress in his absence; Industrial Light & Magic was not off to a good start and had only a few months left to finish the film. Lucas had a lot on his plate, between editing, looping, overseeing ILM, and planning pickups for what he didn't capture during principal photography.

From Lucas's point of view, he would be lucky if his film made its money back. In fact, things looked decidedly grim for the future of his galaxy, which he'd spent a lot of time and effort willing into existence. Consequently this first brainstorming session would indicate that Lucas was thinking of using Foster's second novel as a blueprint for a possible sequel to *Star Wars*. It would be a lower-budget affair, which may be why Lucas starts out the conversation by moving most of the story's action to a planet surface; this film would have fewer visual effects. But Lucas was already determined to continue the life of his characters. Given Lucas's state of mind at this juncture, however— he'd almost had a heart attack not long before—it's more than likely that Lucas was simply hedging his bets.

Nevertheless, their conversation opens a window into Lucas's mindset at the time, and a few things become clear. For example, Lucas thought that Darth Vader was a relatively weak villain, that Leia could run off with a Wookiee and be killed off, possibly, and Luke could become more like James Bond. Remember: This is before James Earl Jones came in and did the voice for the Sith Lord. That would change his persona quite a bit—as would sound designer Ben Burtt's sound effects.

After the film's immense success— a big surprise to everyone—Lucas would opt to re-think the sequel. He'd had a lot more time to mull things over and many things had changed, notably Harrison Ford's decision to reprise his role as Han Solo.

The following is the first of a two-part transcription of their conversation:

THE JEDI WHO FELL TO EARTH?

George Lucas (GL): One remaining thing that I want to cope with is putting the whole thing on the scale of a Western, making the whole thing work as a Western—more of a Sergio Leone Western. It can go more into the middle of nowhere where these really slimy creatures live. Essentially, space can be boring. And I would like to get much more into the *Seven Voyages of Sinbad* [type of thing]. Now we've established the space fantasy, we can move it away from that.

> "ESSENTIALLY, SPACE CAN BE BORING... NOW WE'VE ESTABLISHED THE SPACE FANTASY, WE CAN MOVE AWAY FROM THAT."
> —GEORGE LUCAS.

We're getting down now onto earth and can make it in a different way. It's getting down to something much more like on Mars, so you're running around in a strange world. And we can make Luke much more of a warrior. I'd like to have Luke going on some kind of mission, something to do with the primary plot. He has to deliver the syrup or whatever, something that depends on his getting somewhere. He takes off in his little fighter and he crashes on this planet.

Alan Dean Foster (ADF): Are you giving him an X-wing or a Y-wing?

GL: We can get him an X-wing.

ADF: Is there a Wookiee in this?

GL: We could have a Wookiee.

ADF: I think if you stick him on a desert planet, it would be an awfully funny spot

for a Wookiee. He'd be sweating like crazy.

GL: Well, the original idea [in the rough draft script from 1974] was to have a whole colony of Wookiees. But it does get a little much. There's something attractive about not just having one, but a couple.

One thing is that I'd like to make a new robot. I would like to design a totally mechanical little robot. Before shooting the film, there was no research done at all. Nobody even thought of saying, "Well let's go see a real robot." So I think, now, having been through it once, the essential idea is to try to go with a real robot; I think given the right amount of preparation and research we could make a very interesting little robot.

ADF: What about two of them? An evil one and a good one? You could do all kinds of things, have them fighting each other.

GL: That's possible. One thing that I have to cope with is that it is a sequel. We have two main characters here [C-3PO and R2-D2] that you can't really ignore. I have to go with them in some way. I either have to get rid of them or explain them away or use them. I thought it might be cute to have Artoo just the way he is and then have a little one so that Artoo becomes a sort of big brother and has the little one always hanging around. He's a little antagonist who's sort of bugging Artoo all of the time.

Let's put in, for the time being, that we have Artoo back and we have a third one, a littler one who can be an interesting adjunct.

THE CRYSTAL CONNECTION

ADF: What about if they are looking for something that supposedly magnifies the Force? Which would also explain what Vader and Tarkin are doing running around this same desert world [sic: Lucas hadn't told Foster yet about his decision to kill off Tarkin].

GL: That was one of the ideas in one of the earlier scripts, which was the kyber [sic] crystal: a crystal that amplifies the Force. The whole point of the movie, originally, was that they were trying to get the crystal. The crystal was in the robot and they were trying to get it. Luke was trying

Above: In a humorous moment, Lucas once thought that Leia and Chewbacca's relationship could have taken an unexpected turn.
Opposite page: Luke Skywalker: A cool James Bond-esque figure in the sequel.

> ## "LUKE'S FOUGHT A FEW MORE WARS, KILLED A FEW MORE PEOPLE." —GEORGE LUCAS

to get the crystal back to Ben, who needed it. But something like that is a good—

ADF: Well, it gives Luke something to look for on the planet and it gives a reason for Vader and Tarkin to be there.

GL: I'd like to put a time jump in there of about four or five years from the end of the film. During those years, Luke really grows as a warrior. He has become much tougher. We can even assume that he's had a couple of battles. He's a little more seasoned and a little harder. He's a much tougher guy than he was in the beginning, where he was a goofy kid. That's the transition I wanted to make in the first

movie, but I couldn't make it, primarily because there wasn't enough time to make that much of a bend in his character. So I'd like to make a dissolve in his character, make it a few more years later, with him having fought a few more wars, killed a few more people, become a little sharper, got cheated a few more times, and become a much more worldly character.

ADF: I think you can do that to a certain extent. But I don't think you can make him over. One of the things that's so attractive about Luke is that anybody who ever felt like a klutz in high school watching the football players run around can identify with him. You can't make him over into Clint Eastwood. You can't identify with Clint Eastwood. Clint Eastwood, even though he's the hero in the film, I have no sympathy for him whatsoever. If he got shot at the end of the film, I wouldn't be particularly upset, whereas I would with Luke. Now, Luke has all kinds of reasons already for turning into a tougher character. The baptism of fire and running around with the X-wing and the fact that his parents were killed [sic], which is crucial.

GL: Luke is an agent for the Rebellion, he's a fighter, much more of a hero. He's also much more worldly. We can try to turn that page a little bit. I think it would be a good thing and I'd like to see him grow.

ADF: That's the idea, of course. Given what he learned from Ben and that he was taught by Ben, he grew up to become like Ben, not Clint Eastwood. He's tough, but he still has some vulnerability that everyone can identify with. He's not a hired savage.

GL: We can do his bar scene. The kind of scene where he walks in and the guy says all these terrible things and somebody pulls a gun and Luke gets to [show his stuff.] It's like when you watch James Bond films, we find out this guy is an assassin ready to kill him. Bond knows it and we know it. And we are asking why he's getting into the car if he knows it [as in *Dr. No*]. But it's the bravado. We realize this is a guy who is so good and so cool that he can see the trap, walk into it and come out on top.

LEIA'S CHOICE

ADF: It would be very interesting if Leia showed up on this same planet.

GL: One of the things I thought of is a crash... So they crash together. Or she was already there and she was captured, and he is coming and looking for her, and he crashes... or maybe she was visiting a distant cousin.

ADF: She's already there on a mission of her own and they run into each other; she's incognito, not wearing her princess robes and all of that, and then they run into each other and he doesn't know what she's doing and she doesn't know what he's doing. Maybe they're into the same thing. But we don't know at this point so we can set up a very interesting relationship with her still being very courteous and only Luke has changed. It's a different Luke now and we can have them play off of each other.

GL: Well, we either have them come together or crash together. It's the kind of thing where she went somewhere on a mission, a diplomatic thing to set something up, very sort of underground-y kind of thing with strange people on the planet and she's hasn't been heard from since, so Luke wonders what's happened to her.

ADF: Then you don't use her as much because you can't find her.

GL: Well, he can find her instantly. I mean you've got them both there on the planet. And you have finding her be 25 percent of the script. The rest is another adventure that develops out of this.

I'm still willing to kick things around. Part of it is this relationship, which is, how far have they gone together. We've left them in a very neutral position. We left them where she can run off. Obviously Han is the one who is really hustling. But we don't know at this point which one she picks. So the one thing we can do is answer that question. Obviously, we get into a rough situation if she picked Han. At the end of the first picture they're all standing there wondering whether she and Han will go off into the spaceship and she sort of hangs out with him for a while, and obviously puts Luke out.

ADF: The point is at the end of the picture, the impression I get—and I still am an

outsider to the film—is that the princess is the princess and she doesn't take anybody. It leaves Luke feeling disappointed because he was interested in her, but she is completely unattainable at the end of the picture. She's just as divorced [from Luke and Han] as the other generals standing up there in the throne room. But Luke is not; Luke wants her. That's the impression I get. When she's standing up there hanging his medallion around him, she doesn't try to kiss him or anything.

GL: Well, another thing we could do is to go one step beyond the simple and move into the love story plot, where you have them kind of vying for each other. She is a spry little snappy kind of girl and he's sort

SPLINTER OF THE MIND'S EYE

The Second Star Wars Saga
From the Adventures of Luke Skywalker

by

Alan Dean Foster

Based on the Characters Created By
George Lucas

rev.version: July 77

of liking her, and in the process of the movie, about one or two thirds of the way through, they fall in love and have a wonderful relationship and in the end she gets killed. It's one of those tweaked ideas, but it's one of those things that works. What I wanted to do when we were shooting the other movie is have the princess run off with the Wookiee. But it sounds perverted.

Charles Lippincott (CL): I think that somebody else has got to be killed.

GL: I wouldn't mind killing her off.

WHO'S THE PAWN AND WHO'S THE MASTER?

GL: The other thing that we haven't dealt with is Darth Vader. But Darth Vader

himself, as we discovered in this picture, tends to be pushy; he's not strong enough as the villain to hold the villain role. He doesn't have the persona that you need. You really need a Cushing guy, a really slimy, ugly...

CL: What about if you unveiled him, unmasked him? Since he isn't strong enough to hold up. Unmasked him and started building up a new villain who could continue into the next?

GL: That's an idea.

ADF: A *Phantom of the Opera* scene right there. People will be curious....

GL: Well, we had an interesting idea, which we sort of liked but we didn't do it. Somebody thought we were going to take the hood off of Vader and there was going to be Peter Cushing, this shriveled up old man inside this giant suit. A little of *The Wizard of Oz* idea. That was a fairly interesting idea. The one thing about that, though: Darth Vader is good as he is a real menace. It's just good to have that guy who you love to hate there. So if you use Darth Vader, fine. Or the bad guy is his agent on the planet. It's the local governor, it's the local whoever that Darth Vader is using to find the crystal or whatever he needs....

When you wrote the novelization, you pointed out that Vader was just using Tarkin for whatever reasons. In a way we set up Vader as the pawn. The trouble is [Vader] appears to be the pawn, but Tarkin is the pawn. In the end, it's reversed: Vader appears to be following Tarkin around, but in reality, it's reversed.

ADF: I always thought of Vader as the behind-the-scenes manipulator. I'm not sure of his motives, or what he is, or what he is after, except that he is after evil on a grand scale. Maybe if we kept him that way, didn't unmask him...

GL: We know now that Luke is one of the few white knights, working for the light Force and trying to learn the white Force. If we put in the kyber crystal thing, which is a way of intensifying the energy force....

ADF: You can have them blow up mountains or you can have the local villain have his head be disintegrated!

Continued overleaf!

This page: Ralph McQuarrie's stunning cover art for *Splinter of the Mind's Eye* would go on to become one of the most iconic images from the Expanded Universe. **Opposite page:** The title page from Foster's July 1977 manuscript makes plain Lucas's change of tact, as "The Second" is crossed out. It would not be considered a sequel to the film. "Carol" refers to Carol Titelman, who oversaw Lucasfilm's publishing program at the time.

R. M°QUARRIE

After a break of one week, Lucas, Foster, and Lippincott reconvened on October 20, 1976, for part II of their brainstorming session. In the interim, it would seem that Foster had written up a rough outline based on their first session, so the three of them are riffing off of that as they strive to come up now with the basic story beats.

GL: It seems a lot like the first one. Because in the first one we met the Wookiees in the cantina and we had that cantina fight. I was wondering if we could just turn that around a little bit and do something different, which is, have Leia take [Luke] to the Wookiees or something like that, where the Wookiees show up in a different way and maybe a little bit later. I like the thing with the jail and everything, and having to go and get the Wookiees out.

ADF: Well, you know, I'm always reminded of the scene where they are trying to break Cary Grant out of jail in *Gunga Din* and they are using the elephant and the elephant winds up pushing the whole jail over.

GL: The other thing you've got to remember which is a little tricky, is that the Wookiees can't talk.

ADF: Right, I hadn't forgotten. But they cannot talk English, right?

GL: But they can talk Wookiee talk, yeah.

ADF: That might be kind of fun, too.

GL: I've made some notes on things and I was interested, just stylistically, in getting into a very... Once we reach a point of fusion, which ought to happen somewhere in the first third, everything comes together. It's like in *Star Wars* now, once they get dragged into the Death Star, there is a fusion point and the rest of the film is just simply running around. They are constantly getting chased. It's Flash Gordon from that point on. And I'd like to do that stylistically in this one—to the point where it's even more extreme than what I did in the first one. We can just constantly throw them from one cauldron into another...

ADF: As soon as Luke touches the bit of crystal, he knows Vader is coming. Then it's a race between them and Vader to get to the crystal. And off they go through jungles and mysterious alien civilizations, and you can have the second race of aliens walking around and throw in all of the wonderful jungle effects or bog effects—

GL: It's really creating a tension, reaching a point where, right from the very beginning, they're in trouble.

ADF: Yeah.

GL: And building their problem, so they just get into more and more and more trouble until the end. We have the search aspect of it where they are constantly searching, which is a motivating force, but the whole thing I would like to see is that they are chased the whole way. Not only are they chased, but they are constantly getting into trouble, falling into bottomless pits.

"WE CAN CONSTANTLY THROW [LUKE AND LEIA] FROM ONE CAULDRON INTO ANOTHER." —GEORGE LUCAS.

ADF: *Alice in Wonderland.*

GL: I like the idea, which is interesting and also very classic, of Luke becoming a leader of the tribe kind of thing, your basic hostile tribe. They get captured or whatever, and he has to do hand-to-hand combat with the chief and he wins [something that Annikin Starkiller does in the rough draft, vs. a Wookiee—JWR]. They all...

ADF: ... retreat, heal, and make up.

GL: Yeah. Flash Gordon did it with the cave people or whatever they were...

ADF: Okay, but to what end? So they can help him against Vader?

GL: Yes.

ADF: Okay.

GL: He has to use the tribe. It becomes his army. That was one of the things in the rough draft [from 1974]. He [Annikin] did that. They got captured and he... I went through the whole thing... They get captured by the Wookiees and he does a razzle-dazzle on them and fights the head Wookiee.

WHAT ABOUT SOLO?

ADF: Part of the problem with the Han Solo character is I don't think you can just bring him in in the end.

GL: No, you can't. He has to be in the very beginning. He has to be there.

ADF: Either he's a central character or he's not in it. Because he is that kind of a character and that is a problem, too. You can't make him just a peripheral character. But I don't think you need him anyway; you have Luke and the princess and Halla and the two Wookiees all running around together. You've got five people all running around together. A sixth person is going to become a mob scene.

GL: Yeah, well that's the problem in the first one. We'll let Han be in the second sequel novel. That's better. Where he's the central character and the others are either not there or are very peripheral.

MORPHING MONSTERS

ADF: It might be interesting if the princess suggests that they go hide in there and then they fall down in a hole. It gives Luke an excuse to yell at the princess. Or would you rather have the princess yell—

GL: Well, we did that before in the first one, that constant yelling back and forth at each other. We've got to have a slightly or much more sophisticated interplay between them. It's got to be a much more of a ...

ADF: Carole Lombard and John Barrymore instead of Jean Harlow and Wallace Beery.

GL: Luke and the princess should have one short little adventure before they

get captured. I don't know quite what that should be. I don't want it to be something like a landslide or anything.

ADF: I'll think of something.

GL: Some kind of a problem. Something that has got a lot of energy to it. And of course we just had them fight a monster and we can't really have them fight another one.

ADF: We have to be careful or this is going to be a monster a minute.

GL: Yeah.

CL: You could have the original one. The light one that was down there [in the second draft of *Star Wars*—a kind of Id monster from *Forbidden Planet*]?

GL: The clear monster. [Editor's note: This becomes the "lake spirit" of Mimban in the novel.]

CL: Right. It could be done. It would be much easier to control in a cave.

GL: Well, it was all more or less underground originally.

ADF: Well, I don't know, that's up to you. Tell me what your monster's like.

CL: It could be like a poltergeist.

ADF: It could be very interesting with Luke and his lasersword fighting a light type of creature. You know, the sword contacts the creature and there's a flare of light here and flare of light there. Luke fighting the Id monster [from *Forbidden Planet*] if I got this pictured right.

GL: Well, the idea was that it was much more like a translucent thing, like a big jellyfish.

ADF: Right...

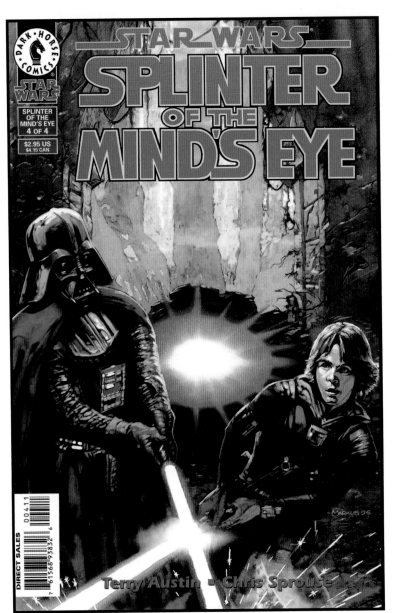

"IT'S A FIGHT BETWEEN TWO EXTRASENSORY GIANTS!"—GEORGE LUCAS

GL: I'd like Luke to pause near some weird plant or something and he jumps into a pod and they are going across this black lake—and then in the middle of the lake something keeps bumping the boat, and it's all that weird *Jaws* stuff. You don't know what's going to come out of the water at you. Something like that you can do in a tank. If you can do it at night, you're free to deal with it however you want. You could have the monster walk across the

water. It could be so ethereal, something that's not really there, but...

ADF: Swamp gas.

GL: Your basic will-o'-the-wisp monster and he has to battle it on the middle of this black lake. It can either be a giant amoeba kind of thing, which is the dynoga [sic]. The more ethereal beast from the Id, which is something that doesn't really exist... that's just something superimposed.

THE OL' TIME-LOCK

GL: One thing that we should do, though, is in the beginning, in the cantina, Halla should say where the crystal is. I think we should say it's at the great temple of Gaga Zoomi or something, so we know that they are going to a definite destination. That's the place they've got to get to. I think it's fairly important to establish that.

ADF: That's where the final big fight scene is.

GL: Yeah. It's a time lock. Essentially, you're saying the movie is going to be over when they reach this place. It's just a matter of getting there. Obviously, when you get there there's gonna be a big battle. It's that simple. I like the idea of the battle, which I was going to do in the first movie [Luke duels Vader on the surface of the Death Star in one script—JWR]. But when we got into the Death Star, it wouldn't have really worked out very well.

The good thing about being in a temple is that you have a lot of junk around. So it's not only a sword fight, but a fight between two extrasensory giants, where Vader can pick things up and throw them across the room.

GIVE ME A STATUS REPORT, CAPTAIN PIETT: HOW LONG UNTIL WE ACHIEVE ORBIT AROUND CIRCARPOUS IV?

Opposite page page: Luke and Vader duel on the cover for issue #4 of Dark Horse Comics' *Splinter of the Mind's Eye* adaptation.
Left: Vader cuts an imposing figure in the Dark Horse adaptation, but George Lucas originally had other plans for his most iconic character.

We also wanted to have a scene where Vader goes and bows before the Force and the Force picks him up and tells him that he better go out and get that crystal... But it's not the Force personified; it's on the verge of personification. Maybe it's a shadow or something.

ADF: The ultimate...

GL: It's the ultimate evil. It's the devil.

BUILDING UP VADER

GL: You mean kill the Wookiees?

CL: Have Vader kill them; they run into Vader first.

GL: Possible.

CL: You could really build this whole thing on the threat of Vader.

GL: Poor Wookiees. I haven't killed

"I HAVEN'T KILLED ANYBODY IN THIS STUFF YET. OH, I GUESS I KILLED BEN." —GEORGE LUCAS

anybody in this stuff yet. Oh, I guess I killed Ben. I forgot about that.

CL: Vader killed two people in the first movie. He choked that one guy to death. But the point is have him kill somebody sympathetic again, to help to build him up as a villain.

ADF: Well, we're both thinking the same thing; I don't want to kill the Wookiees. It works already.

GL: A real problem that we have in the first one is creating a threat out of Vader. I mean he never does anything to anybody.

I mean, he chokes one guy.

ADF: He talks tough.

GL: Yeah, but he really doesn't do anything. So it'd be good that we actually see him do some evil things. Or you know what else we can do? Might be a little hokey, but let's say we arrange it so that something... so that Luke is caught somewhere on something. We get to the temple or whatever and they go for the crystal and Luke gets trapped in some kind of fiendish device. A big rock comes down on his toe or something and he's straining to pull himself loose. And then Vader shows up and says, "Oh, now I've got you." And the princess is forced to fight Vader. Luke is standing there trying to pull his toe out and Vader knocks her down.

ADF: He's playing with her really.

GL: I think she could desperately fight him but he is really overpowering and beats her up pretty bad and...

ADF: Another reason to hate Vader.

GL: Yeah. Rather than having him cut her in half, she just gets pummeled about a lot. Although it wouldn't be too good to have a bloody freak in the movie. But she's pretty much battered up. She's sort of dragging herself around on the floor in really bad shape and finally Luke jumps down and starts on Vader. And Luke kills Vader in the end. I was thinking of the last image of having her be this bloody, battered, beat-up babe. Not very romantic. I don't know whether I dare do something quite that extreme. We could have the last image be them getting into the spaceship and taking off, flying into the sunset.

ADF: I like very much the idea of Vader beating her up and cutting her up. And then Luke gets the sword from her at the last minute and Vader is about to cut her head off or something, and Luke kills Vader. And then Luke uses the crystal to heal the princess. Everybody breathes this big sigh of relief. That will make everybody feel real good.

GL: It's a little strong, but I'm willing to go with it.

ADF: I don't think it's too strong. He's not bringing her back from the dead.

THE REAL VILLAIN

ADF: Anyway, Luke encounters Vader there and kills him. What happens at the end? Do they keep the crystal? Is Luke going to keep this crystal? Is he going to give it to some local people who deserve it? I think it would be wonderful, after all this fighting, if someone drops the thing and breaks it.

GL: That's always, for me, very disappointing. I think it would be fun if he just kept it. He has it and it makes him go up one more level... A little halo appears around his head.

ADF: Well, not Superman.

GL: Oh, no no no. He just goes from level 2 to level 3.

ADF: Maybe we could have something interesting, visually. I want something more than just: Vader's dead and Luke pulls the crystal from the eye of the idol.

GL: He takes the big crystal down and it glows and he looks into it and he sees Ben Kenobi.

ADF: Ben Kenobi, yes. And everyone in the audience can have a flicker of recognition from the first movie. Would you want to do it, though?

GL: Hmm... No. It's a little hokey. The whole thing is that it's about the Force, which I have a tendency to avoid. With Luke killing Vader, standing there with his severed head and his sword stuck in his gut—that's the heroic image in the end—David and Goliath. Goliath is dead and David is standing there. But the overtone of it all is that there will be another [villain] soon. So he's got the crystal but the crystal will only help him fight the Force, which is even bigger than Vader. It just gives him one more little weapon to use against the the evil Force,

the dark side of the Force. You hold it on a shot—it's the Frank Frazetta moment —of Luke holding the princess and the crystal in one hand and the sword in the other and the princess is holding on to him.

ADF: And the natives are cheering.

GL: And he's got the foot on Vader.

ADF: You want a voice thundering through the room or something?

GL: No. A little thunder clap or something. ☺

Thanks to Pablo Hidalgo for his input.

┌─**EXPANDED**──────────
│ Follow J. W. Rinzler
│ on twitter @jwrinzler
──────────**UNIVERSE**─┘

This page and opposite: The climactic duel between Luke and Vader from the Dark Horse adaptation.

STAR WARS
INSIDER

SPECIAL 150TH ISSUE!

FIRST LOOK!
DARTH VADER'S HOT WHEELS!

THE CLONE WARS **LOST MISSIONS EPISODE GUIDE!**

LEGO LEGENDS
15 THINGS YOU NEVER KNEW ABOUT LEGO *STAR WARS*!

ISSUE #150
U.S. $7.99
CAN $9.99
JULY 2014
Please display until July 21

TITAN

0 74808 01805 5

50

ROGER CHRISTIAN
SET DECORATOR/ SECOND UNIT DIRECTOR

ISSUE 150
JULY 2014

My first contact with Roger Christian came when I was called to interview him at County Hall on London's South Bank. There was a large *Star Wars* exhibition opening, showcasing assorted props, costumes, and even a life-sized Naboo N-1 fighter. Roger had a great deal to say about his time on *Star Wars*, describing the creation of the lightsabers and Luke's landspeeder. He even told how he, as second unit director, was the first person to shoot new footage for the first *Star Wars* movie in 16 years, *The Phantom Menace*. Over the years, our paths have crossed on numerous occasions. Roger's long lost short film, *Black Angel*, which ran before European prints of *The Empire Strikes Back*, was rediscovered in 2014. A surprisingly influential and evocative piece, the film gained a new audience when released on iTunes, leading to a full-length remake being prepared for release.

It should be noted at this stage that Roger has something that all interviewers hope their subjects will have: a perfect recollection of events. Think about it: Can you recall exactly what you were doing, in detail, from over 30 years ago? It's testament to Christian's vivid recollections and his unswerving loyalty to the saga that we have such an intriguing insight into the *Star Wars* movies.—**Jonathan Wilkins**

Roger Christian was born on February 25, 1944. He has worked as a set decorator, production designer, and feature film director on numerous projects including Alien, Monty Python's Life of Brian, *and* The Young Indiana Jones Chronicles. *He received an Academy Award for his work on the original* Star Wars *and was Oscar-nominated for his work on* Alien. *Christian's feature films include* The Sender, Nostradamus *and* Battlefield Earth.

THE MYTH MAKER

ROGER CHRISTIAN WON AN ACADEMY AWARD FOR HIS SET DECORATION ON 1977'S INAUGURAL *STAR WARS* BEFORE WORKING AS SECOND UNIT DIRECTOR ON *RETURN OF THE JEDI* AND *THE PHANTOM MENACE*. *STAR WARS INSIDER* CATCHES UP WITH THE GREAT MAN FOR AN EXCLUSIVE ONE-TO-ONE. WORDS: CALUM WADDELL

Artist-turned-filmmaker Roger Christian boasts a hugely creative stint in fantasy cinema that includes Oscar-winning set and prop design work on *Star Wars* and a similar role on 1979's groundbreaking *Alien*. At the time of *A New Hope*, Christian was a young, aspiring artist who had worked on such television series as *My Partner the Ghost* and *Jason King*—but a chance meeting with director George Lucas would seal his fate and, ultimately, bring him into the fold of the hit franchise.

"There were only a few of us that really saw what George was doing with *Star Wars*," begins Christian. "There was the set designer, John Barry, and Nick Maley on effects, and we would have lunch together every day. We became quite good friends during that time. But not everyone was behind George. I remember the cinematographer on *Star Wars*, Gil Taylor, gave him a really hard time—and he was not the only one. There were others who thought it was just a cheap sci-fi film being made for children. It was just a job for a lot of the people on the set. Before *Star Wars*, sci-fi was considered the lowest ebb in cinema. George changed all that and sci-fi suddenly had a big, Oscar-worthy endorsement. I think *Alien* helped as well. Both of these films made sci-fi sexy to a new, younger audience. But, before that, the budgets were small and no one took this sort of cinema seriously."

STARTING OUT

As a central part of the design team, Christian was also sent out to faraway locations in order to scout possible whereabouts for eventual Lucas landscapes. The desert scenes of *Star Wars* were shot in Tunisia—although the artist reveals that Morocco was originally in the running for some sequences....

"I had been to Morocco before," he reveals. "It was a place I really liked. I actually used to visit the country a lot when I was younger. I remember sitting on a slip of canvas, strung across three oil barrels, while I was scouting for *Star Wars* locations. It was very dusty and some of the country was still quite desolate. I remember saying to George, 'I think all of this wind and dust might cause some problems.' John Barry had filmed a movie called *The Little Prince* in Tunisia a few years before so he steered

"I THINK SIR ALEC GUINNESS WAS THE REASON GEORGE SURVIVED THE WHOLE THING!"

Star Wars towards there. Morocco had a much more ancient feel, but Tunisia worked out better because Barry knew the area so well."

Christian also has fond recollections of the *Star Wars* cast, whom he insists also supported a frequently exhausted Lucas during the globe-spanning shoot....

"I think Sir Alec Guinness was the reason George survived the whole thing," adds Christian. "As I mentioned, Gil Taylor was not very nice to him—and I will say that gently. There were huge arguments on the first day, and that continued, and people joined into Gil's camp—such as John Stears, who worked on some of the special effects. The rest of the cast was great though—and as soon as they saw Alec Guinness taking it seriously they all worked hard, too. Harrison knew George from *American Graffiti* and he was the cement, if you like, between Lucas and the other actors. It was Mark Hamill's first film and he was putting everything into it. Carrie Fisher was the same. A lot of these memories came back to me when I was about to do *The Phantom Menace*. Rick McCallum asked me to come up and meet him and George about directing the second unit. I remember George said, 'There were only about five key people on my crew during *Star Wars* who stuck by my side.' Then he said that I was one of them. But I saw what George was doing. I grew up absorbed with old legends such as King Arthur and stuff like that— these are what got me through my childhood. When I read the *Star Wars* script I could see that it was not just another throwaway sci-fi movie— I saw what was under the surface."

Main image: Design director Doug Chiang and Roger Christian work with Ahmed Best (Jar Jar Binks) and a pit droid both of which will later be replaced by digital versions of the same characters.

Below, from left: Feeling the heat in the Tunisian desert; Christian in the *A New Hope* production offices; sharing a joke with Ahmed Best on *The Phantom Menace* set.

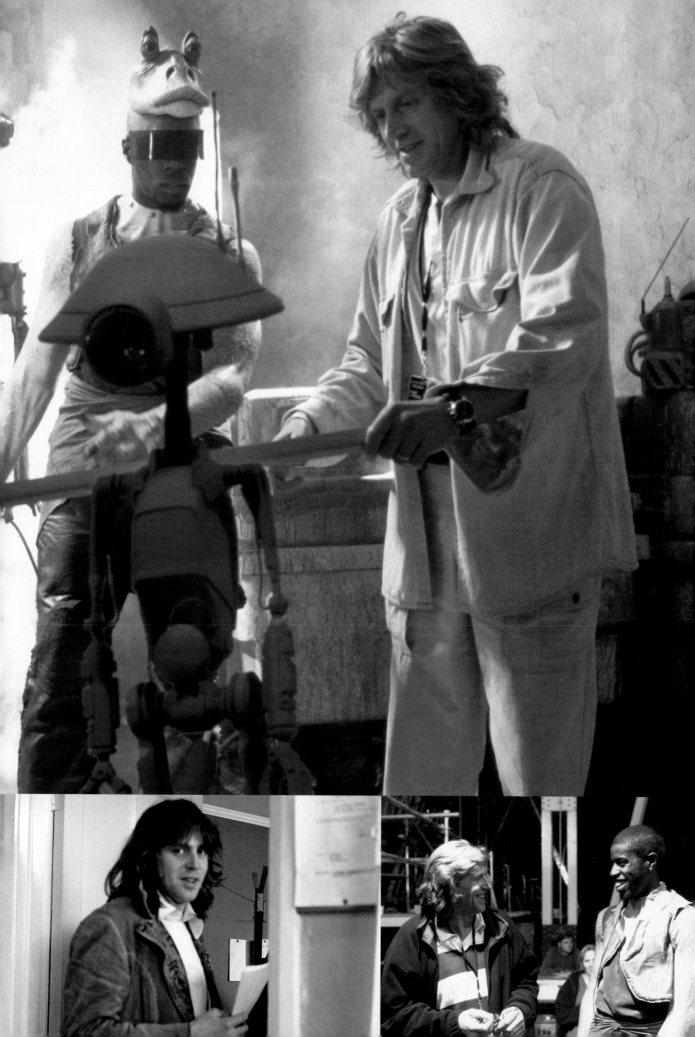

"GEORGE'S TARGET WAS ALWAYS THAT YOUNGER AGE GROUP. I AM NOT SURE HE EXPECTED THE DADS AND GRANDADS TO BE SO ENTHRALLED BY IT."

INTO THE DIRECTOR'S CHAIR

Certainly, Christian's loyalty towards Lucas, and his belief in *Star Wars*, paid off when his first filmmaking effort, the acclaimed 25 minute short *Black Angel*, was given a spot before *The Empire Strikes Back* when it first played in UK cinemas. Visually mesmerizing, the gothic beauty of *Black Angel*—which was shot in Scotland—has recently been re-mastered and shown to considerable acclaim at numerous film festivals.

Moreover, Christian was given the responsibility of directing second unit on both 1983's *Return of the Jedi* and 1999's *The Phantom Menace*...

"I had just designed *Alien* and I was determined to move into directing," says Christian. "I was offered the chance to design *The Empire Strikes Back,* but I really wanted to stick to my ambitions. Finally I got the chance to do my own short film, *Black Angel*, which George wanted to show before *The Empire Strikes Back*. He even said to me, 'Once you have finished this— please make sure I am the first person that gets to see it.' I wanted *Black Angel* to seem like an old classic myth, an ancient legend from another time. Then George brought me back to direct six weeks of second unit on *Jedi*, which was

great because in that role you don't carry the weight of being the guy in charge. I just did what George asked and had a really fun time—although a lot of my job seemed to be spent filming Ewoks! George had me shooting all of the Ewok parties and stuff like that. I remember thinking, *He obviously plans to make a standalone movie about Ewoks at some point,* and I was right! I think he could see that they were going to appeal to a young audience."

Of course, the Ewoks continue to be a source of some contention for older *Star Wars* fans—but Christian maintains that the series was always designed to be family-friendly and the ardent adult following was never something that Lucas anticipated....

"George's target was always that younger age group," he mentions. "I am not sure he expected the dads and granddads to be so enthralled by it. That's how Jar Jar Binks came about as well. People might forget this, but the kids loved Jar Jar when *The Phantom Menace* was released. It was just the adults that couldn't stand him [*laughs*]. But George always said he was making *The Phantom Menace* for a young audience."

Another source of controversy, of course, is that *Star Wars* now exists only on the Blu-ray market in its Special Edition, with additional scenes and CGI effects added to the classic 1977 template. Christian admits that he would like to see the original cut out there as well—while understanding the reasoning behind the numerous alterations that have been made...

"George is just an inherent fiddler," he laughs. "But he does maintain that he would have done all of these added sequences if the technology had been there back in 1977. I do think it would be a good idea to put out the original *Star Wars*, untouched, for fans. Just as a separate edition. Maybe that will happen eventually now Disney have the property—I don't know—but, at the end of the day, George wanted people to see the film that he always wanted to make. I sort of understood putting in

the Jabba the Hutt scene. That is how *Star Wars* was written, and intended, but the money and expertise just wasn't there. I know as a filmmaker myself that I always want to fiddle with my films afterwards. At the time, when you are making a movie, you are under such pressure that you think, *Oh dear, I wish I hadn't let that happen.*"

Now a director in his own right, with a CV that includes the paranormal horror gem *The Sender* (1982), the well-regarded biography *Nostradamus* (1994), and the epic *Battlefield Earth* (1999), Christian continues to remain a huge fan of fantasy filmmaking. As such, he mentions that he remains interested in what will happen next in the *Star Wars* universe....

"J.J. Abrams is obviously a very good filmmaker," enthuses Christian. "I have heard that he is going back to the feeling of the original *Star Wars* from 1977. I think that is a relief because George managed to present a mythic quality to that film— it was something that really tapped into your subconscious. Underneath all of the space ships and lasers it was a film adapted from ancient stories and legends.

"I think that is the enduring legacy of *Star Wars*: It is a space Western, but it is also a myth. I hope that still gets retained. But I guess we will all have to wait and see!"

EXPANDED

Follow Roger Christian on twitter @roger_christian
Black Angel is now avaliable on iTunes.

UNIVERSE

PRINCESS DIARIES
CARRIE FISHER SPEAKS OUT!

BRING ON BANE!
AN ALL-NEW TALE INSIDE

STAR WARS
INSIDER

CAUSE FOR
CELEBRATION!

INSIDER SALUTES:
- ✴ 5 YEARS OF *STAR WARS: THE CLONE WARS*
- ✴ 10 YEARS OF *ATTACK OF THE CLONES*
- ✴ 35 YEARS OF *A NEW HOPE*

ISSUE 136
OCTOBER 2012
U.S. $7.99 CAN $9.99

TITAN

JOE JOHNSTON
VISUAL EFFECTS

ISSUE 136
OCTOBER 2012

THIS MONTH, FAR, FAR AWAY....

The Clone Wars: "The Soft War" aired

Star Wars: The Clone Wars: The Complete Season Four released

Star Wars: Agent of the Empire Volume 1—Iron Eclipse released

Star Wars: Dark Times Volume 5: Out of the Wilderness released

The Clone Wars: "Tipping Points" aired

Star Wars: Who Saved the Galaxy? released

The Walt Disney Company agrees to acquire Lucasfilm Ltd. for $4.05 billion and announces new *Star Wars* to be released, starting in 2015

Star Wars: Darth Maul—Death Sentence 4 released

One of the greatest contributors to the look and style of the *Star Wars* universe is Joe Johnston, an incredibly talented artist/designer whose work really gave George Lucas's movies a great sense of visual continuity.

This interview came to *Insider* via Thomas G. Smith, whose book *Industrial Light & Magic: The Art of Special Effects* offered an insightful, in-depth look at the pioneering work of the company—rare in books of that time.

Johnston is interviewed here just after the making of *Return of the Jedi*, a talented craftsman still only 33 years of age. It's easy to forget just how young the crew of *Star Wars* generally were. At this stage in his career, Johnston was six years away from directing his first full-length movie feature, the hugely successful *Honey, I Shrunk the Kids*. It was this success that led to a number of features including cult favorite *The Rocketeer*, stylish horror melodrama *The Wolfman*, and the smash hit *Captain America: The First Avenger*.—**Jonathan Wilkins**

Joseph Eggleston "Joe" Johnston II was born May 13, 1950. He started his movie career as a concept artist and effects technician on the first Star Wars *film, before becoming art director on one of the effects teams for* The Empire Strikes Back. *He became one of four people to win an Academy Award for Best Visual Effects for his work on* Raiders of the Lost Ark. *Johnston continued to work on many films as an effects expert. He was also associate producer on Lucasfilm's fantasy* Willow, *and served as production designer on the Ewok TV movies in the mid-1980s.*

Johnston also wrote and illustrated the children's Star Wars *storybook,* The Adventures of Teebo: A Tale of Magic and Suspense.

In 1984, George Lucas gave Johnston a paid sabbatical in order for him to attend the USC School of Cinematic Arts.

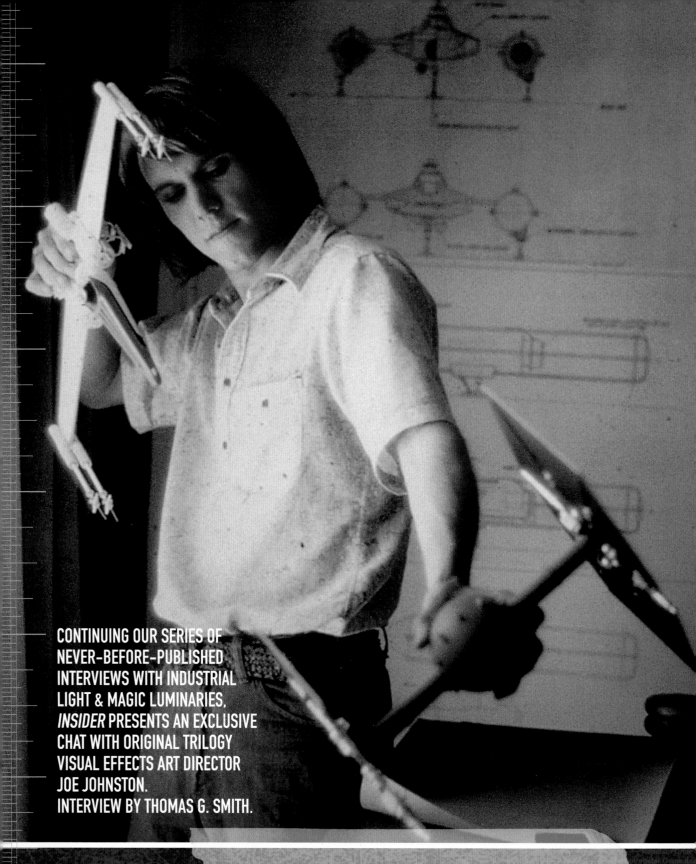

CONTINUING OUR SERIES OF
NEVER-BEFORE-PUBLISHED
INTERVIEWS WITH INDUSTRIAL
LIGHT & MAGIC LUMINARIES,
INSIDER PRESENTS AN EXCLUSIVE
CHAT WITH ORIGINAL TRILOGY
VISUAL EFFECTS ART DIRECTOR
JOE JOHNSTON.
INTERVIEW BY THOMAS G. SMITH.

JOE JOHNSTON:

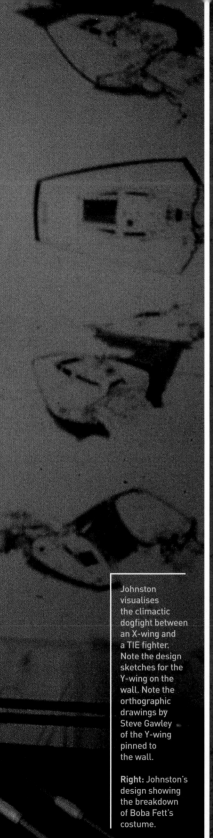

Johnston visualises the climactic dogfight between an X-wing and a TIE fighter. Note the design sketches for the Y-wing on the wall. Note the orthographic drawings by Steve Gawley of the Y-wing pinned to the wall.

Right: Johnston's design showing the breakdown of Boba Fett's costume.

Thomas G. Smith: What were you doing before you worked with George Lucas?
Joe Johnston: I was working at a place called DesignWorks. Chuck Pelly, who was a pretty well-known product designer, hired me straight out of school to work in his design office. I had to get up at 6:30am and leave Long Beach to get to Malibu for about 8am. It was great when I got there, but it was a miserable drive. I worked there for a week and I decided on the following Monday I was going to tell him that I just couldn't do it anymore. I was making $250 a week and it just wasn't worth it. Fortunately, that Thursday night, I got a message from Bob Shepherd, who I had worked for on a Paramount project that was kind of a remake of *War of the Worlds*. He said, "Come on up on Saturday and interview for this, if you're interested. It's a space movie and we're just starting to assemble people. It's gonna be an interesting team and a good project." So I went out that Saturday and then the next Monday I was able to tell Chuck that I had a better offer—having made $250 a week, I thought that $300 a week was an amazing raise!

What year was it you went to work for George Lucas?
It was August 1975. Ralph McQuarrie had been hired and had done five or six paintings. John Dykstra [visual effects supervisor] was there; he actually hired me. I didn't meet George until about a month after I'd been working doing storyboards. Richard Edlund [director of visual effects photography] was there and a couple of machinists.

Were you given a script of *Star Wars* and told to start storyboarding?
There was a script. I don't really remember working from the script, but I recall sitting down with Dykstra and having meetings, going over storyboards and shots. We were really just tossing ideas back and forth. The opening sequence was the first thing I started on: the Star Destroyer flying over the camera, and the laser battle, that kind of stuff.

When did you get a chance to talk to George?

He came up to the art department in early September. The department consisted of a room about the size of one of the sound stages—it was a huge room—and in one little corner of it was a little drawing table and a couple of places to pin up things. I was the only artist working there. George just came through and said, "Hi, how are you doing?" He didn't even introduce himself. It wasn't until we went over to Verna Fields' garage—where I guess she had just finished editing *Jaws*— that we sat down and went through the dogfight sequence. It was George's personal cut [using WWII and old film footage] of the sequence.

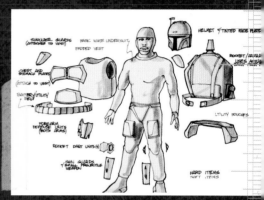

What was the first ship to be designed?
I think the first ship that I redesigned (because all the stuff had been designed by concept sculptor Colin Cantwell in model form) was the Star Destroyer. There were six or seven ships that had been designed and we kind of kept the general shape of a lot of those. We had to change things for technical reasons, mostly. I think that's a really interesting design, but you could never photograph that. It didn't look enough like a battleship: it looked like a fortress or a minelayer.

So what was the atmosphere like around that time?
Well, nobody knew exactly what they were doing; that's the way I remember it. Dykstra and Shepherd and some of the machinist guys had worked on *Silent Running*, but most of us didn't really know what we were doing. We didn't come from film backgrounds. We were just trying

A Design for Life

things that we intuitively thought would work. Sometimes they didn't and sometimes they did.

What did you think about the possibility of the movie being a success?
I didn't really think it was going to be a success until we started seeing sequences assembled toward the end. We watched them in our little screening room with six rat-infested couches. We could never get it completely dark in there; we'd close all the blinds we could and see it without sound on a projector that wasn't always running correctly. It was fantastic. That's when we started thinking it was going to be okay.

Six weeks before the film came out, we were supposed to be on some little film magazine, and got bumped for something else. George said, "Look, when this movie comes out I promise you that it'll be on the cover of something. Something about this film will make it." It was the understated expectation of the year.

What kind of things do you think of to obtain the quality for a good picture in a movie?
You have to give people something interesting to look at. It doesn't matter if it has that much to do with the story; if there's something entertaining on the screen, it can even be just something that moves, that's the primary consideration. It kind of comes down to something intuitive: a nice camera move, make the ship do something interesting, put a nice sweeping turn in there. Everybody notices a frame that's flat and dull. If there's nothing to look at, your eye wanders all over the place.

In what way do you induce dimension?
In designing the shot, you can only imply dimension. When the shot is cleared out and it's executed, there are all kinds of ways to do it: color the thing in the foreground as opposed to the same fade color in the background, aerial haze or just lines of perspective. It's like doing a painting; ways to lead the viewer's eye into what you want them to look at. It's just basic drawing, basic composition: If you have a picture with a guy who's standing there and pointing, people are going to look away. It's the same thing: Getting people to look at something, leading their eye into the frame, and telling them what to look at.

Does George know exactly what he wants before he talks to you?
Not all the time. Sometimes he'll ask for a design for something and explain what he needs it to do: "It has to do this: Two guys need to ride on it and they have to

blow up something." Sometimes he just says, "Give me something to make an exciting vehicle or spaceship for these guys." Sometimes he's not even that specific.

What were the instructions for the speeder bike?
I think the only thing he said was that it should be like a landspeeder motorcycle, something for one man to ride on. That was as far as he went. He hadn't designed or really thought about the whole bike chase sequence too much. The only thing

I remember him saying repeatedly was, "They need to fly through the trees, dodging around and they need to look like they're going 200 miles-an-hour." It later became 80 miles-an-hour.

What does George bring to a project that makes it what it is?
He has vision. Even though lots of people from different departments are contributing to that vision, he's able to convey what that vision is. He's able to guide people very easily, not only because he's articulate, but because he has a way of inspiring people.

What kind of things does he look for?
He looks for unique, exciting, interesting, and off-the-wall designs. He likes things that don't look like they *should* work, but you feel *could* work. Most of the ship designs are just different. All of the designs are unique. Trying to come up with something that hasn't been done before is the hardest thing to do, but he's able to do it. People say, "That looks like something from *Dune*," or "That looks like something from *Buck Rogers*." Well, it may, but it's the way it's treated and used that really makes it unique. Everything's been done before, but George

SCHOOL OF *GALACTICA*

After *Star Wars* wrapped, many of the ILM crew worked on the original TV series, *Battlestar Galactica*. Johnston recalls: "*Battlestar Galactica* was like school for a lot of people working on it. It advanced the technology beyond *Star Wars* up to almost the point of *Empire*. I think on *Galactica* there was a shot that had 25 elements in it, which you could never do on *Star Wars*."

OPENING BIG

Joe Johnston on the opening shot of *A New Hope*:

It blew everything away. It was such a great way to start a film and it caught the audience off-guard. Everybody thought, *Oh, here's a nice starfield and here's a nice little planet. What's going to happen? Is there going to be a nice little ship that comes in slowly?* People were expecting a *2001* shot and then… It's like the Indians attacking a stagecoach in space. That was a good example of forcing people to look at something: This giant thing coming overhead with very strong perspective lines. It was just a good design. That whole opening sequence was really George's idea; he knew exactly how he wanted it to work. I'm sure he must have played that sequence in his head 100 times, because when he was describing it, he knew precisely what he wanted it to look like.

> ## "GEORGE ALWAYS SAYS, 'JUST COME UP WITH SOMETHING INTERESTING, MAKE IT NEAT, MAKE IT FUN, AND THEN WE'LL WORRY ABOUT HOW TO DO IT!'"

somehow finds a way to do it better and differently.

How has technology changed things for designers?
It's not only the design, but also how that design relates to technology. Maybe, in the past, movie crews had the ship sitting from right to left because they couldn't right focus correctly, or they had no way of getting enough depth of field to bring it to camera. With the development of the Dykstraflex motion-controlled camera and the technology that has come along in the last 10 years, designers have been able to be more creative. It's a real good example of

design and technology working together. It's kind of rare.

So because of the motion control, you can just envision anything and it can be done?
That's the way George likes to work. He always says, "Don't worry about how we're going to do it. Don't worry about how much it's going to cost. Don't worry if it's impossible to do. Just come up with something interesting, make it neat, make it fun, and then we'll worry about how to do it." He doesn't like to limit himself by budget or any kind of technical restrictions in the concept phase and I think it shows. For a lot of directors,

that would be the first thing they'd worry about. If you come up with a really great idea that works, you'll come up with ways to make that idea work to budget.

If you could only show somebody one movie that you worked on, which one would you feel best about?
I think that would probably be *The Empire Strikes Back*. I think that was a good mix, but it still had a lot of the spirit of *Star Wars*. It was technologically advanced enough over *Star Wars* to be a lot more fun for me. Looking at the three films back-to-back, *Star Wars* looks real crude. The action sequences are slow. Even when the ships are flying 100 miles-an-hour, they just seem slow.

Empire combined that spirit of experimentation and not really knowing if something was going to work or not—I'm talking about the crew now—with a big leap in technology. I had a lot more responsibility on *Empire* than I did on *Star Wars*. I was one of the people that George brought up first; I was able to get a jump on it and design a lot of things along with Ralph McQuarrie early on. I had a lot of time to show it to George. It was really a luxury as far as the design phase. It didn't really work out that way on *Star Wars* or *Jedi*. On *Jedi*, the responsibility was kind of diluted between the American crew and the English crew. The English crew had a lot more input on *Jedi* than they did on *Empire*. I just enjoyed *Empire* more. It was more fun than *Jedi*.

After *Star Wars*, producer Gary Kurtz said, "The next one's going to be a lot easier. We know how to do it. We can do it in half the time and it's going to

be much easier." Was that the case? *Empire* was harder than *Star Wars*. Technically we were able to do more, so we wanted to do twice as much. We didn't want it to be easy; we wanted to make it go as far as it could. *Jedi* was the same way, but for some reason it didn't work as smoothly.

Can you tell me a little bit about the process of designing a creature for the film?
Taking the Ewoks, for example: a lot of times, George feeds us just enough information to point us in a direction. The first thing he said was, "They're little furry guys, they carry

spears, and they run through the woods." We did 300 drawings of little furry guys running through the woods. A lot of them were troll-like or gnomes and all kinds of little things. Maybe some of them had cute little faces, puppy-dog faces. He picked the puppy dog one and said, "That's looking pretty good. Do some more like this. Make them cute." After a while, I kind of picked up on the direction he was heading and I did one so cute, it looked like the teddy bear's picnic. It had little ears and was wearing a little bonnet. George came in the next day and said, "That's it! We'll kill 'em with cuteness! Try them all cute. We might as well go all the way since we've been heading in that direction. Let's make them like little teddy bears." ⟁

Below: Richard Edlund (director of special effects photography), John Dykstra (special photographic effects supervisor), George Lucas and Joe Johnston. (ILM coordinator Patricia Rose Duignan is in the background.)

FASTER, MORE INTENSE!
Joe Johnston on speedy ships:

I remember when we were in the moviola room working on *Return of the Jedi*, and George was looking at a shot and said, "No guys, this has got to go faster: I've been telling you! Look at *Star Wars*! It has to go faster." We'd heard this for about four days in a row, and the ships were getting so fast that in four frames—they were gone! So somebody got out reel 4 and reel 7 of *Star Wars* and ran it. There was silence for a minute and then George said, "Huh, kind of slow isn't it?" The impression was of tremendous speed, but the audience's impression of speed doesn't have to be like hyperspace—you just establish the scale of the ships. The opening of *Star Wars* seems very fast because that ship is so big. You know how big it is, the size is implied, but it's not really going that fast.

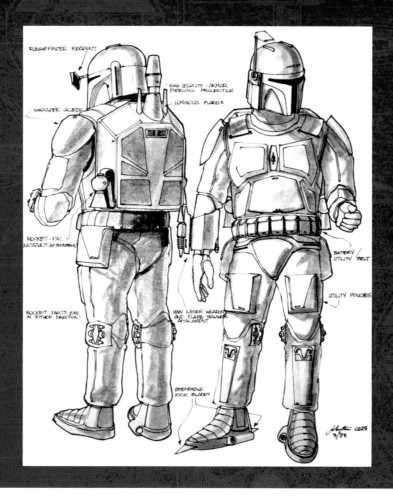

RANGEFINDER READOUT

HIGH VELOCITY - ARMOR
PIERCING PROJECTILE

SHOULDER GUARDS

LUMINOUS FLARES

ROCKET-PAC
NOZZLES (EXTENDABLE)

BATTERY
UTILITY 'BELT

UTILITY POUCHES

ROCKET PARTS (FIRE
IN EITHER DIRECTION)

MAIN LASER WEAPON
AND FLAME THROWER
ATTACHMENT

EXTENDABLE
KICK BLADES

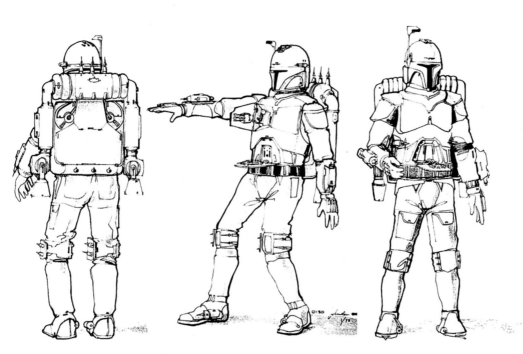

EARLY SKETCHES OF ARMORED SUIT FOR SUPERCOMMANDO.
LATER BECAME BOBA FETT.

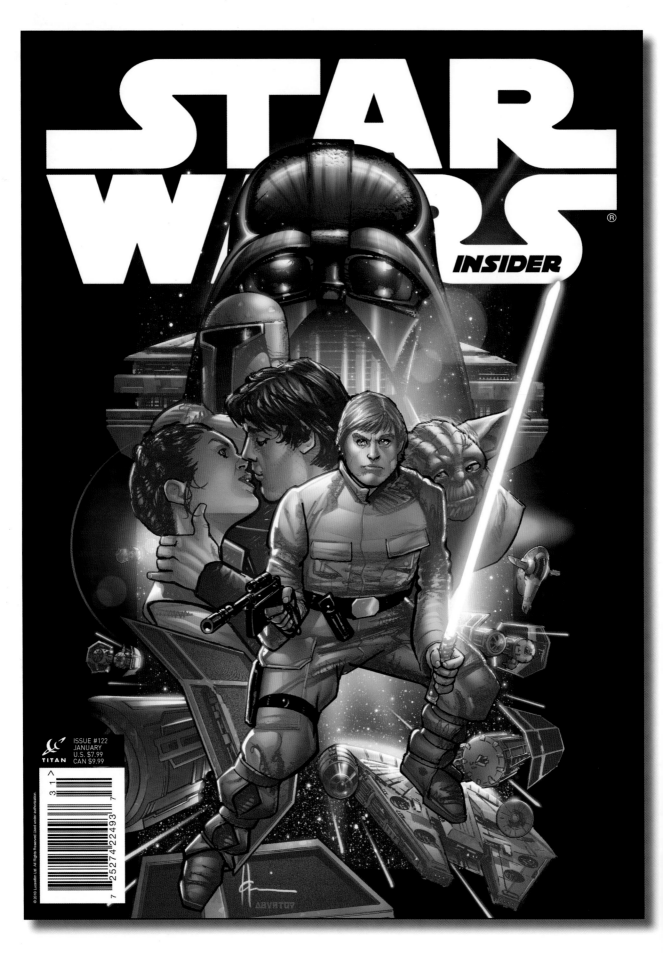

STAR WARS

INSIDER

ISSUE #122
JANUARY
U.S. $7.99
CAN $9.99

TITAN

GEORGE LUCAS
CREATOR OF *STAR WARS*
AND
HOWARD CHAYKIN
MARVEL *STAR WARS*
COMIC BOOK ARTIST

It's a fascinating thought, that, in today's world of secrecy and embargoes, both the novelization of *Star Wars* and the first four parts of Marvel's *Star Wars* comic book adaptation were made public before the first movie was even released into cinemas.

The conversation you are about to read shows the creative process involved in planning and creating a comic book version of a movie. What's particularly fascinating is that George Lucas is involved, taking a keen interest in planning the comic.

It's testament to their efforts that Marvel's *Star Wars* was such a hit that it is often credited as helping Marvel through a difficult time. The comic book series provided a springboard to an extremely successful ongoing series, instrumental in establishing an expanded universe of offbeat stories and characters.

To tie in with this issue, *Insider* commissioned Chaykin to revisit his original San Diego Comic-Con poster, creating his take on *The Empire Strikes Back*. Typically stylized, it proves that we must get around to having him complete the classic trilogy.—**Jonathan Wilkins**

Howard Victor Chaykin was born October 7, 1950 in Newark, New Jersey. He graduated from Jamaica High School in 1967, and in the summer of 1968, worked at Zenith Press. He attended Columbia College in Chicago that fall, but left school and returned to New York the following year. After high school, he hitch-hiked around the country before becoming, at 19, a "gofer" for the respected comic-book artist Gil Kane, whom he would later name as his greatest influence.

ISSUE 122
JANUARY 2010

THIS MONTH, FAR, FAR AWAY....

The Clone Wars: "Grievous Intrigue" aired

The Clone Wars: "The Deserter" aired

Rebel Force: Trapped released

The Clone Wars: Day One released

Star Wars: Knights of the Old Republic Volume 8: Destroyer released

Star Wars: Dark Times 15: Blue Harvest, Part 3 released

Star Wars: Knights of the Old Republic 49: Demon, Part 3 released

The Clone Wars: "Lightsaber Lost" aired

Crosscurrent released

Star Wars: Legacy 44: Monster, Part 2 released

The Clone Wars: Decide Your Destiny: Crisis on Coruscant released

The Clone Wars: Decide Your Destiny: Dooku's Secret Army released

The Clone Wars: Stand Aside - Bounty Hunters! released

The Clone Wars: Holocron Hunters released

The Clone Wars: "The Mandalore Plot" aired

MOVIE FRAME TO COMIC

PARTICIPANTS:

Artist Howard Chaykin

Editor Roy Thomas

Writer-director George Lucas

Marketing and merchandising
vice president Charley Lippincott

BE A FLY ON THE WALL AS GEORGE LUCAS CHATS WITH ARTIST HOWARD CHAYKIN AND EDITOR ROY THOMAS ABOUT ABOUT ADAPTING HIS MOVIE TO THE FOUR-COLOR PAGE. WORDS: J. W. RINZLER

O n July 27, 1976, just 11 days after *Star Wars* wrapped principal photography, writer-director George Lucas met with comic book artist Howard Chaykin and Marvel comic book editor Roy Thomas. Their goal: Begin a collaboration that would result in the very first comic books based on *Star Wars*.

The trio of Lucas, Chaykin, and Thomas had been brought together by Charley Lippincott, Lucasfilm's marketing and merchandising vice president. He had already hired Chaykin to illustrate a *Star Wars* poster that was sold at sci-fi and comic conventions in advance of the film's release.

At this point in the making of the film, barely a single special effects shot had been completed by Industrial Light & Magic.

Twentieth Century-Fox, the studio that was financing *Star Wars*, entertained little hope of making its money back and was actually trying to divest itself of the movie. Even Lucas was feeling very depressed about his space fantasy—the shoot had been a horrible experience. So, all things considered, it was a minor miracle that Lippincott had managed to score a contract with Marvel— a premiere comic book publisher—to adapt Lucas' script into a six-book series. Three of those six were scheduled to appear on newsstands before the film's release in order to heighten comic book fan awareness.

For years, the transcript of this key conversation lay buried in a box in the Lucasfilm Archives. *Star Wars Insider* presents highlights of this discussion for the very first time.

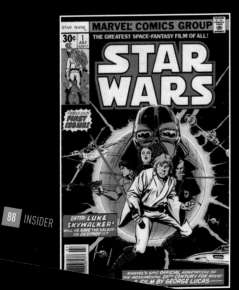
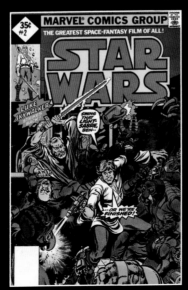
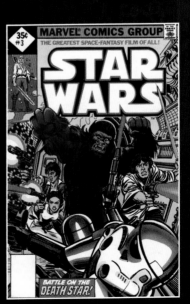

FRAME: THE GENESIS OF THE STAR WARS COMIC BOOK!

This page: Howard Chaykin's take on the *Star Wars* heroes. Previous page: The first four issues of the adaptation, three of which hit stores before the movie was released.

George Lucas: Well, I think this is just primarily to meet you. I'm a big fan of yours.

Howard Chaykin: Thank you. It's nice to be accepted.

Lucas: [I've] got a lot of your stuff. Especially your *Cody Starbuck* [a swashbuckling space pirate, whose comic book adventures began in *Star Reach* #1, 1974]. About halfway through [creating *Star Wars*], I discovered Cody Starbuck and it's great. That's what I like. It's fun. I like the style.

Chaykin: I could do with it whatever I wanted to do. I'm looking forward to getting started on this thing.

Lucas: What do we want to get out of this, Charley?

Charley Lippincott: We're going to talk mainly about visual stuff. Have you thought anything about the visual style of the book?

Chaykin: Not to any great extent. My only reasons for wanting it to be a black-and-white comic book were that reproduction was getting to the point where

LucasFilm PRESENTS: ROY THOMAS, SCRIPTER/EDITOR ★ HOWARD CHAYKIN, ILLUSTRATOR ★ JIM NOVAK, LETTERER ★ ...ADAPTING THE GREATEST SPACE-FANTASY OF ALL!

STAR WARS

ADAPTED FROM THE *GEORGE LUCAS* FILM, A *20th CENTURY-FOX* RELEASE

It is a period of CIVIL WAR in the galaxy.

A brave alliance of UNDERGROUND FREEDOM FIGHTERS has challenged the tyranny and oppression of the awesome GALACTIC EMPIRE.

To CRUSH the rebellion once and for all, the EMPIRE is constructing a sinister new BATTLE STATION. Powerful enough to destroy an entire planet, its COMPLETION will spell CERTAIN DOOM for the champions of freedom.

Striking from a fortress hidden among the billion stars of the galaxy, REBEL SPACESHIPS have won their first victory in a battle with the powerful IMPERIAL STARFLEET. The Empire fears that ANOTHER defeat could bring a THOUSAND MORE star systems into the rebellion, and IMPERIAL CONTROL over the galaxy would be LOST FOREVER.

BUT, THAT IS THE NEAR FUTURE.

AT THIS MOMENT:

ABOVE THE YELLOW PLANET TATOOINE, A GIGANTIC IMPERIAL STARSHIP PURSUES A REBEL SPACECRAFT--ITS DEADLY LASER BOLTS DISINTEGRATE THE SMALLER SHIP'S MAIN SOLAR FIN WITH A SOULSEARING SHUDDER...!

MARIE SEVERIN, COLORIST

Ben "Obi-Wan" Kenobi prepares to meet his destiny. Above: The dramatic opening page of the *Star Wars* comic book adaptation.

black-and-white is best. I could see why you want it in color, of course.

Lippincott: I think it's Marvel, too. We've talked about it back and forth.

Chaykin: All reproduction in comics is incredibly inconsistent, but it's less inconsistent in black-and-white. For the kind of comic book it's going to be, I think color would probably be best. I'll do it in a fairly illustrative style and we'll see how the first one runs. I still want to keep it very simple. You're going to have to bold it up a little bit, because the fine line just isn't reproducing.

I'm still trying to figure out how I'm going to do the laser swords [lightsabers]. I have no idea. I think I'll just have to get down and do it, mess it up a couple of times before I get it right. It might have to be done with color.

Lucas: That'll be great. We're looking forward to it—our wonderful adventure in comics. We all hope. It'll be interesting to see how it goes with the movie.

Chaykin: Are there going to be any problems with likenesses?

Lucas: Well, I don't know. That's another thing. How do you feel about that? Do you feel comfortable with attempting likenesses or would you rather avoid that completely?

Han and Luke: Hard-faced heroes!

Chaykin: Are any of your actors going to be—?

Lucas: No, no problems.

Chaykin: Okay, because that's come up often. I'm going to attempt likenesses, only a simplified likeness. I mean over a single book, I could probably do it; over six issues, it's going to be a royal pain.... Simply because no matter how many photographs you give me—you could give me tons—and it still wouldn't be enough, because there are just so many shots of heads.

I feel that kid who plays Luke [Mark Hamill] is a little soft in the face, so I'm going to harden him up a little bit. He's got a great cleft and that's fine, but he looks like he's 16. It'll make him more heroic in the picture. Han Solo is perfect. He looks like I drew him. He looks a mercenary hero—he looks like Starbuck. Alec Guinness is no problem, he reeks character. Chewbacca will be no

LUCAS: THE FIRST COUPLE OF ISSUES YOU'RE GOING TO HAVE TO SKIP ALONG MERRILY!

problem. Same thing is true of Darth Vader. Darth Vader is a comic book character. He looks like a comic book character—Doctor Doom.

I will need considerable material on the hardware. I've got all the material I need on the guns. I need plenty of material on the X-fighters and the Y-fighters, much more than I have now, if there is any available.

Lippincott: I've got color prints of the models, of the X-wing and the Y-wing.

Chaykin: And I need the interiors on the Death Star. I have absolutely no idea what it looks like.

Lippincott: That's a problem. There are no good shots.

Chaykin: I need the interior cockpit shots and stuff like that, also some color guide. I had no idea what color to use for Han Solo's outfit, his hair; the Princess; I suspected Luke was blond, but it could have been sandy hair. Various things like that. My only key was the paintings [by Ralph McQuarrie]. I'm glad I don't have to get started yet.

NEITHER HE NOR THE DISTRACTED TROOPERS HAVE SEEN FIVE FORMS RACING TOWARD THE CAPTURED STARSHIP...

WHERE IS THE DATA YOU INTERCEPTED?

W-WE'RE ON A DIPLO-MATIC MISSION--!

LIAR! WHERE ARE THOSE INFOR-MATION TAPES?

THIS SHIP CARRIES THE CREST OF ALDERAAN! IS ANY OF THE ROYAL FAMILY ON BOARD?

Darth Vader, who Chaykin felt resembled Doctor Doom, makes his presence felt!

DARTH VADER, DARK LORD OF THE SITH, TIGHTENS HIS FINGERS ON THE REBEL OFFICER'S THROAT.

BUT, HE STILL RECEIVES NO ANSWER...

Chaykin: I need head shots on all the major characters and the minor ones. I have no idea who Biggs is, the other pilot. The general in the war room with the Princess, I don't know him.
[Roy Thomas arrives]
Lippincott: We were talking about style a little bit, the illustration work.
Roy Thomas: The writing will follow the screenplay, with a few captions that we'll put in. "Suddenly—" for example.
Lippincott: An occasional "Suddenly." There's a lot of "Suddenly" in the script.
Thomas: Yeah, I know.
Lucas: "Suddenly this," and "Suddenly that."
Lippincott: We put a few in the novel. We put a few in today.
Lucas: We added one to the novel. He didn't have any "Suddenlys!" Have you figured out at all how you're going to break it down?
Thomas: No, we haven't really discussed that. But we will—
Chaykin: Before we start. We'll just figure that out first.
Lucas: Because I haven't the foggiest idea how it's going to work.
Chaykin [to Thomas]: What I'd like you to do, because I'm leaving Thursday, is read it and get some vague idea of how you want to do it. And drop me a line and tell me.
Thomas: Oh, yeah, I will. You mean when you're back East. Well, before we begin we'll figure out about where we'll be in terms of space.

I just don't want to fake anything.
Lippincott: If you wanted stuff that was color-keyed—
Chaykin: Well, I won't have to color the books. The first issue isn't due on the stands until February [1977] and that means they're due [for completion by] December. By then, I hope to have all the books penciled, at least, and most of it inked. I hope to have the whole bunch finished by December or January. So that's cool. So I can spend January coloring six comics. So that's no rush on that.
Lippincott: Where's Roy?
Chaykin: Are you sure he knows he's supposed to be here? I'd like to have him read that script, and break it down for me.

LIPPINCOTT: SOME PEOPLE IN THIS TOWN STILL THINK IT'S THE BATTLE BETWEEN STARS AT ONE STUDIO AND STARS AT ANOTHER.

Lippincott: But he needs a new script. That's another reason for coming over here today. He mislaid the script I sent him. [To Lucas] Are there any changes now since that script [the fifth draft, or shooting script]?
Lucas: A little bit of ad-lib went on.
Chaykin: It's going to be a lot of fun to do. There's a lot of material to work with.
Lippincott: If you want to look at footage tomorrow, we can do it in the morning.
Lucas: Actually, if they're going out to [ILM], they can also see the models.

EVEN AS THE TOWERING CHEWBACCA FLATTENS THE STARTLED OFFICER WITH A SINGLE BLOW, ANOTHER "IMPERIAL TROOPER" APPEARS AT THE DOORWAY...

GAROOO!

WHUMP!

ZZK!

--TO BLAST THE ONE WITHIN, BEFORE HE CAN REACH HIS OWN WEAPON!

But everybody back East who has seen the collection of materials—people have all gone nuts. The reaction has been incredible. Because at first, it was like, "Come on, one more? Who wants another crummy science fiction movie?" When they see the material, they can tell. Scientists in particular, they know there's something for a start. All the guys at the studio want sets of those paintings.

Lippincott: What logo are we using?

Thomas: There's a couple of good ones. But I was wondering, do you have a regular logo that will be well-known by the time [the film is released] or are we free to design our own if we—

Lippincott: We'll be in the process of designing one. I know Twentieth [Century-Fox] wants one.

Lucas: Yeah, it's hard to know whether we should let them go ahead and do what they want, because the one we've got is essentially the company logo, the one on the T-shirt.

Lucas: It's also tricky, because it starts slow and builds, so you've got to be really... The first couple of issues, you're going to be really scraping to try and make something happen, or you're going to have to skip along—merrily.

Lippincott: Why? The first issue's got that whole capture of the ship.

Lucas: That's right.

Lippincott: And by the second one, you've got the robots being hunted down. You've got something in there that's built-in for a comic. I don't think there's a problem.

Lippincott: Howard, what about the sky battle [over the Death Star] at the end? How do you think we can solve that?

Thomas: You mean the impersonality of the whole thing? Well, there are shots in the cockpit—the way you do it in a film. Again, that'd be a graphic problem. Inset panels, shooting back and forth. We've got plenty of room. That's the good thing. It's going to be part of a continued story, and by the last issue or two, where this is happening, [the readers] will be pretty well into it and we'll be able to afford an issue of that type.

Lucas: Your basic "Fighting Air Force" issue. Well, at least we have a variety of ships. We're not stuck with one or two kinds.

Chaykin: Right. That kind of stuff can get real dull real fast. As long as there are interesting designs on the ships. Because the ships streaking—one goes by, and then after that it begins to get a little boring.

THEN--
YOUR POWERS ARE WEAK, OLD MAN!

YOU SHOULD NEVER HAVE COME BACK!

SZRAK

YOU... ONLY KNOW... HALF "THE FORCE"... VADER...!

YOU PERCEIVE ITS FULL POWER... AS LITTLE AS A SPOON... PERCEIVES THE TASTE OF FOOD!

YET, EVEN AS THEY FIGHT, BEN SEEMS TO BE UNDER IN-CREASING PRESSURE AND STRAIN--AS IF AN INVISIBLE WEIGHT WERE BEING PLACED UPON HIM...

HE MAKES A SUDDEN LUNGE AT HIS FOE --

ZZHARP

--BUT IS CHECKED BY A LIGHTNING MOVEMENT OF THE TOWERING ARMORED GIANT!

that. Alec Guinness was pretty good with a sword, but the guy who played Darth Vader [David Prowse] was terrible [at sword fighting]. Alec Guinness wasn't a swordsman, but he still could do it. And getting them to actually be good at it was really—

Lippincott: The still pictures are horrible.

Chaykin: Well, I will choreograph the swordplay [in the comic].

Lucas: The other thing is that it's hard in real-life, especially if you aren't a swordsman to actually get it to work.

Chaykin: That's one thing I will idealize. ☮

Thomas: I know they'd be kind of reluctant to use that. It's a little hard to read on a newsstand when a kid's looking to buy it. We'd probably be best off if we made something simple—a two-line thing. It's no longer "THE *STAR WARS.*" You never called it "THE." I thought you dropped something?

Lucas: Yeah, we dropped it.

Thomas: I think just putting those two words [together]... we ought to put a line above the title, too—kind of a lead-in. You know, like "Frenzy in a Far-Flung Future," that kind of thing. You know, if there is something like that that might go well above the logo in addition, some lead-in, something or other that ends in the words *STAR WARS.*

Lucas: We're still looking for that.

Lippincott: Some people in this town still think it's the battle between stars at one studio and stars at another.

Thomas: Well, I guess it could be.

Lucas: They think it's the Elizabeth Taylor-Richard Burton story.

Thomas: There's a little confusion with using that against the *War Wizards* [Thomas is referring to the Ralph Bakshi film, whose title was eventually shortened to *Wizards,* and which came out in February 1977].

MANUAL!? ARE YOU INSANE? YOU CAN'T HIT A TARGET TWO METERS WIDE WITHOUT THE COMPUTER!

BLUE FIVE, ARE YOU THERE? COME IN, BLUE FIVE!

THE YOUNG SPACE-PILOT DOES NOT RESPOND -- UNLESS IT IS BY PUSHING A BUTTON ON THE CONTROL-PANEL BEFORE HIM --

Lucas: The style of the [*Star Wars*] poster was very Kung Fu, which is very popular, but it really read Kung Fu more than anything. In the movie, it is a very Samurai [thing]; it's much more Samurai.

Chaykin: Well, the sword seemed too long to use as a rapier.

Lucas: No, it is a Samurai [style sword]. You don't really see it work that often in the film. Only when Ben and Vader have their fight; that's the only time you see it in any kind of a fight. Hopefully, in the future, I can begin to make Luke into much more of a swordsman. But ultimately there just wasn't room in the picture for it.

Thomas: Particularly when the climax is the space fight.

Lucas: Well, also in the sword choreography, it got very difficult, it always does in a situation like

THEN, WITHOUT WARNING-- THE ETERNAL NIGHT OF SPACE BECOMES, FOR A FEW SECONDS, THE BRIGHTNESS OF DAY!

NO ONE DARES LOOK DIRECTLY AT THE EXPLODING BATTLE-STATION-- --NOT EVEN MULTIPLE SHIELDS SET ON HIGH COULD DIM THAT AWESOME GLARE SUFFICIENTLY TO PREVENT PERMANENT BLINDNESS.

THE UNIVERSE SEEMS FILLED FOR AN INSTANT WITH TRILLIONS OF MICROSCOPIC METAL FRAGMENTS, PROPELLED PAST THE RETREATING SHIPS BY THE LIBERATED ENERGY OF A SMALL ARTIFICIAL SUN.

THE COLLAPSED RESIDUE OF THE DEATH STAR WILL CONTINUE TO CONSUME ITSELF FOR SEVERAL DAYS--

--FORMING, FOR THAT BRIEF SPAN OF TIME, THE MOST IMPRESSIVE TOMBSTONE IN THIS CORNER OF THE COSMOS.

STAN LEE PRESENTS: **STAR WARS** — THE GREATEST SPACE FANTASY OF ALL!

CONTINUING THE SAGA BEGUN IN THE FILM BY GEORGE LUCAS

NEW PLANETS, NEW PERILS!

THE DREADED *DEATH STAR* IS NO MORE... AND THE EVIL *DARTH VADER*, ITS SOLE SURVIVOR, IS FLEEING ACROSS THE *GALAXY*, LOST FROM THE SIGHT OF MEN. *

AND, ON THE FOURTH MOON OF *YAVIN*, OLD FRIENDS SAY FOND *GOOD-BYES* WHICH CAN NO LONGER BE *DELAYED*:

GRONK!

*THANKS, HAN... AND CHEWBACCA! BUT YOU KNOW I'VE GOT TO STAY *HERE*...AT LEAST TILL WE CAN SCOUT UP A *NEW WORLD* TO BECOME THE *MAIN REBEL BASE.*

ONCE *DARTH VADER* ESTABLISHES CONTACT WITH THE *EMPIRE* AGAIN, THE YAVIN SYSTEM WILL NO LONGER BE *SAFE* FOR US.

THE *REBELLION* MUST CONTINUE *ELSEWHERE*... EVEN WITHOUT YOU, HAN.

WELL, S'LONG, LUKE... YOU *TOO*, PRINCESS.

I STILL WISH YOU WERE COMING *WITH* US, KID-- YOU'D MAKE A HELLUVA *STAR-HOPPER.*

*AS SEEN IN LAST ISSUE'S *CONCLUSION* OF OUR ADAPTATION OF THE *FILM.* --ROY.

STOP *SNIVELING*, ARTOO! YOU'LL SEE *MASTER SOLO* AGAIN.

BLOOP

ROY THOMAS & **HOWARD CHAYKIN**
WRITER/EDITOR   ARTIST/CO-PLOTTER

FRANK SPRINGER
EMBELLISHER

JOE ROSEN | CARL GAFFORD
LETTERER | COLORIST

ARCHIE GOODWIN, CONSULTING EDITOR

HE SURE *WILL!* WHATEVER YOU *DO*, LUKE-- WHEREVER YOU *GO*-- I'LL *FIND* YOU ALL AFTER I'VE DONE WHAT I'VE GOT TO *DO*.

THAT'S A PROMISE FROM *HAN SOLO!*

SPECIAL EDITION

STAR WARS

INSIDER ®

Special Edition 2010
US $14.99
CAN $15.99

TITAN

 INTERVIEW SPECIAL

RICK MCCALLUM
PRODUCER *STAR WARS* PREQUEL TRILOGY

INTERVIEW SPECIAL
NOVEMBER 2010

THIS MONTH, FAR, FAR AWAY....

Trade edition of Star Wars Art: Visions released

Star Wars: The Old Republic 5: Blood of the Empire, Part 2 released

The Clone Wars: "Evil Plans" aired

Star Wars: Knight Errant: Aflame 2 released

The Clone Wars: "Hunt for Ziro" aired

Star Wars: Dark Times Volume 4: Blue Harvest released

The Clone Wars: "Heroes on Both Sides" aired

Star Wars: Blood Ties: A Tale of Jango and Boba Fett 4 released

Irvin Kershner passed away

Fate of the Jedi: Vortex released

Sometimes you have to really chase an interview to make it happen. It took three attempts to get Rick McCallum, the producer of the *Star Wars* special editions and the *Star Wars* prequel trilogy.

The reason for this was that he was in the process of shooting *Red Tails*, Lucasfilm's World War II movie, in Prague. Attempt one was abandoned because he was busy on the shoot. The second call came just as he was recording his daughter's first steps. When we finally spoke, a week later, he was happy to talk at great length, waxing lyrical about his time on the movies, being fabulously indiscreet, and telling numerous tales, only some of which could be included in the interview.

Because of his candor, I felt I was able to ask slightly more probing questions, such as what he thought of George Lucas's controversial decision to alter Han Solo's confrontation with Greedo in the Cantina.
—**Jonathan Wilkins**

*Born in Germany on August 22, 1954, **Richard "Rick" McCallum** began his career as a producer, working with the respected author, Dennis Potter. During the 1980s he worked with a variety of filmmakers, including Neil Simon, Harvey Fierstein, Nicolas Roeg, and David Hare. Like George Lucas, he worked with the Rolling Stones, producing their video* Undercover of the Night *(Lucas was a cameraman on the* Gimme Shelter *concert documentary). His first role for Lucasfilm was producing weekly live-action television series,* The Young Indiana Jones Chronicles. *Shot in 35 countries, the show featured an impressive roster of directors such as Bille August, Nicolas Roeg, David Hare, Mike Newell, Deepa Mehta, Terry Jones, Simon Wincer, and Carl Schultz. The Academy of Television Arts & Sciences honored* The Young Indiana Jones Chronicles *with 12 Emmy Awards. The series debuted on DVD in 2007, with McCallum serving as executive producer, creating 94 real world documentaries that accompany the episodes.*

I'D TAKE THE
THE
OF

CREW INTO HEART A VOLCANO IF I COULD!

PRODUCER RICK MCCALLUM PLAYED A VITAL PART IN GETTING GEORGE LUCAS' EPIC SAGA TO THE SCREEN, WORKING ON BOTH THE SPECIAL EDITIONS AND THE PREQUEL TRILOGY. WORDS: JONATHAN WILKINS

How did you first meet George Lucas?

Robert Watts [an associate producer of the original trilogy] introduced me to George in 1984 on the set of *Return to Oz*. Robert was showing him around, and he saw us filming on an adjacent stage. We wanted to be on his set, because we wanted all the toys, the cranes, and everything else. George wanted to be on our set because it was an 18-crew film that was shooting in three weeks—the grass is always greener! Later, when I came to work with George, Robert said I'd love it, and he was absolutely right.

You worked on *Dreamchild* and *The Singing Detective*. Do you ever miss working on smaller projects?

I like them both. It's always great to do a big movie, but in many ways, I prefer working on small movies, because they're much harder to make. There's no room for error. We have to do in as little as three weeks what a big film has up to 50 weeks to do.

I like working in television, too. I'd only done a couple of television shows before I did *The Young Indiana Jones Chronicles*. I had done *The Singing Detective* and a film with David Hare called *Heading Home*. You were given a license to fail at the BBC, which was incredibly inspiring and incredibly liberating. You just tried to make the best thing that you could possibly do, and hoped it would be controversial enough that your peers and friends would like it.

Star Wars is so huge. It's hard for most people to understand how big it is. We don't have $200 million to $300 million to make a movie. The films are totally financed by Lucasfilm. We do all the marketing, all the publicity, all the trailers, all the behind-the-scenes, all the making-of [material], and we have to do it for maybe two-thirds less than what others are doing theirs for.

We've got to do more visual effects. On *Star Wars*, we shoot in up to seven countries, and we shoot in 55 days. Other films shoot for up to 120 days. We have to deal with the question of how to bend the technology to help support the film in a way that you can make it in concert with the way everybody else makes a movie. Those are the real differences between *Star Wars* and some other big films.

Has making the *Star Wars* films been the biggest challenge of your career?
Every film is a challenge! It's a series of compromises as you face egos, pride, stars, cast, lack of money, and the weather. All those are there to haunt you and break up this incredible vision that you have in your mind's eye of what the film can be. That's what happens on every film.

Were you ever concerned about making changes to classic movies that so many people knew every single frame of?
Absolutely. I was thinking, *If it ain't broke, don't fix it.* It was ultimately up to George. He had a booklet filled with notes of what he couldn't achieve based on the budget and the circumstances around the original shoot. He never got to be able do the things that he wanted to do, and was never really happy with the way a lot of the material turned out. The films were only a fraction of what he wanted them to be. That's the beautiful thing about film, especially if you're a writer-director and especially if it's a very successful film; you can go back. He wanted to have his version of the film the way that he'd always wanted it. It wasn't up to us to say no to him.

Where do you stand on the changes involving Han Solo shooting Greedo?
I think, for George, there's a second gunman, somewhere in the back near the sandy knoll! It's a conspiracy. It's definitely a controversy with fans, but it's very clear in the original script that [Han shooting first is] the way it was supposed to happen.

Rick McCallum and George Lucas in Tunisia.

Sharing a joke with visual effects supervisor John Knoll as George Lucas prepares Natalie Portman to run the gauntlet of the droid factory in *Attack of the Clones*.

Do you think he might ever go back to that original version someday?

I don't think so, but you'd have to ask him, because there's no such thing as him not tinkering. At that particular time, it was the 20th anniversary, and Fox was desperate to get the film out to a new generation of people who'd never had the chance to see it on the big screen. George looked at his notes and decided to make the improvements. I saw his original notebook with the first version of the script, and everything we changed was in there, marked: "This is what I want to do."

What was the most unexpected challenge of the Special Edition project?

I don't think any of us could have predicted what bad shape the original *Star Wars* was in. It was nobody's fault; Fox had done the very best in terms of storing the film underground, and at the right temperature. But it was truly one of the most tragic things I have ever gone through. I'll never forget, I sat with the head of post-production at 20th Century Fox, Ted Gagliano, and we almost wept. It was just unbelievable that a film that young could already be so totally destroyed. From that moment on, there was never going to be an issue for us about digital technology, and being able to restore as many films as we possibly could, or supporting anyone who wanted to, but also making sure that the very nature of what is America's contribution to the world is protected. It still hasn't happened, but it's slowly happening.

So it was a watershed moment for digital technology?

There are issues with digital, too. Digital must always be completely backed-up to the newest version on the newest server, but it has a greater shot at surviving than film, because film is alchemy; it's living and breathing and it changes.

Taking an urgent call on set!

Two occasional "Sith Lords" take a break from filming at Lake Como!

On the set of *Attack of the Clones* with Ewan McGregor, George Lucas, and Ahmed Best.

Hayden Christensen, Rick McCallum, George Lucas, Natalie Portman, and Ewan McGregor contemplate bringing back "peace to the fans" on the set of *Revenge of the Sith*!

When the three films were re-released into cinemas, they were incredibly popular. Were you surprised?
No. I remember seeing the trailer with *Independence Day*. It was around two minutes long, and *Independence Day* started right after it. You couldn't hear anything for the first 10 minutes of the movie! People went completely bonkers for *Star Wars*!

There were a lot of people in the industry who were totally betting against the Special Editions. We'd sold a zillion copies of the movies on VHS. Why would anybody pay to see it? There was a great guy, Tom Sherak, who was head of distribution at Fox. He rented a five-ton truck and filled it with all the letters that parents had been sending to Fox for years saying, "Why won't you re-release the films in the theater?" The original audience had started having kids, and now they were in their teens their parents were telling them about this incredible experience that they had. I think that was the turning point for George, he said, "OK, we've got to do this."

Is good humor an important trait of a producer?
Well, for me it is. I have a lot of friends who are miserable when they're making a movie, because most of time they're in the studio system, so they have no real power. I don't mean power for power's sake; they just don't have an identity.

I've always been blessed with the work I've been able to do in England and more importantly with George. He knows what a producer does, and lets me have full rein.

We love their movies, we love their shirts. McCallum and George Lucas.

It's my job to turn around and terrorize people when needed. Every producer can be a Sith Lord—sometimes in disguise, sometimes not. They often have to be able to get people to do things they didn't think they can do.

What were the craziest rumors you heard about the making of _The Phantom Menace_?
The rumors themselves came out of the ability to communicate across the Internet, which was fairly new at that time. We heard Charlton Heston was going to be a Sith Lord! It was just absurd, but sometimes it felt so real, I'd read it and think, _I'd better just check with George!_

After the storm destroyed the set in Tunisia, did you ever get close to shutting the film down?
No, I would never let that happen. That's why we have insurance adjusters! Everything was destroyed, except for the staircase leading up to one of the ships. Sets that had taken us 14 weeks to build were all destroyed. There had never been a storm like that. It was basically a hurricane that lifted engines that weighed two or three tons, and moved them hundreds of yards.

Luckily, the Tunisian army was doing maneuvers about 40 miles away, and I got them to help us. We rebuilt everything in the course of a week. We were right on schedule, right on time, and it cost the insurance company a fortune!

You've been quoted as saying that when you're on location you "Never know what's going to happen, and I like that, I much prefer it." Did that experience change your mind?
No, because I love it. I prefer going on location, because the cast and crew becomes a little community. It's like

Good news! Rick McCallum hears the box office results for the first weekend!

Calling the shots on _The Young Indiana Jones Chronicles._

Dark times. Surveying the scenes after a storm wrecked the Episode I set.

Sin City, only you get to control it—or you think you control it—but you don't. It's my favorite thing. I would take the crew into the heart of a volcano if I could—it's more fun.

In Tunisia, it was 135 degrees every day. It meant that you have to figure out if you truly are the person that you think you are. That's not just for me, but for everybody. You become totally dependent on each other. It's like going to war, only luckily you're not going to get hurt. When one person does not fulfill his obligations, it can be very challenging.

The prequels were cast with more established names, compared with the original trilogy. Was that a conscious choice?
Not really. In the 1970s, only industry people read *Variety* or were really keyed into casting decisions for a movie that wasn't coming out for years. You didn't have *Entertainment Weekly* and you didn't have entire cable networks devoted to celebrity programming back then. In the middle 1990s Ewan McGregor and Natalie Portman, who were just at the start of their careers, were already famous, because of the new general interest in all entertainment news.

Was there anything that got cut that you were particularly sad to see go?

Making history as a familiar figure arrives on the prequel set at last!

Preparing and approving designs for *The Phantom Menace*.

A press conference at the Caserta Palace (the Theed Royal Palace) marks the arrival of *The Phantom Menace* crew!

There was an undercurrent to Episode III, where Anakin suspected that Obi-Wan and Padmé were fooling around with each other. We shot scenes of dialogue that hinted at that, but, in the end, it just wasn't right for the film.

The droid factory sequence in *Attack of the Clones* was a late addition to the movie. Does this add extra pressure?
George doesn't start out saying, "Okay. This is exactly what I want to do." He has to write it first, which he says is always painful for him, then he has to shoot it. But then when he takes it to the editing room, which is really what he loves more than anything, then he likes to play with it, and add more stuff to it.

We always have enough time in our pickups to be able to do what we always expect out of George, which is the unexpected. He likes to start a conversation the same way, whether he's in the editing room or when he comes on the set. Part of you wants to groan, but it's thrilling and it's electric. He will say, "Wouldn't it be a great idea if we did this..." or, "You know, I was thinking about it last night; wouldn't it be fun to do this...?" or "People would never believe it if we did this...?" or, "Wouldn't it be great...?" That's how he likes to talk, and then you just say, "Oh, okay, fine, let's do it!"

Which was the hardest prequel to make?
Attack of the Clones. It was the biggest risk because we decided to do every single thing digitally, from acquisition and shooting the picture, all the way to distribution. There was no plan B. We just had faith that it would work.

When I'm doing a film with George, we're always in sync about the casting, and the storyline, but when he first told me the story of Episode I, I thought, *Oh my God, he's lost his mind!* He looked at me and said, "I know you think I'm losing my mind, but this is the only way the story works for me. This is the way I always started off and this is the way it's going to happen. I know older kids are going to hate it, but I know there's another generation," and he was absolutely right.

Those three films have grossed close to $3 Billion, which is a serious amount of people, who saw the films over and over again. On a certain level, we brought a certain amount of peace back with *Revenge of the Sith*, in that the boys that started off as eight when *The Phantom Menace* was released were 18 when *Sith* came out. They were in high school, ready to go to college. They've seen the dark side in their school and their relationships with their girlfriends, their friends and everything else, so that movie was ready for them. I think older fans got to see what they always wanted to see, which was the moment when Anakin turns into Darth Vader. I think that's where they would have loved the films to have started. But that wasn't what George wanted to make, and ultimately he was right. ☮

CLONE CHAT
WITH ROB COLEMAN AND DAVID ACORD!

MERCENARIES
ZAM WESELL AND AURRA SING MATCH-UP!

LAUNCHPAD
ALL THE LATEST NEWS, GAMES, AND FUN!

STAR WARS

INSIDER

C-3PO

ACTION STATIONS!
The Making of a Star Wars Action Figure

MIDAS TOUCH!

C-3PO ACTOR ANTHONY DANIELS TALKS CONVENTIONS & *CLONE WARS*!

ISSUE #107
Feb/Mar 2009 $5.99

BLASTER!
Books, Toys, Collecting,
Classic Scene, Comics,
Ask Lobot, Bantha Tracks!

AN EWOK ADVENTURE
We look back at
1984 and a return
to the Endor Moon

ROB COLEMAN
EFFECTS SUPERVISOR

When *Star Wars: The Clone Wars* launched in 2008, one of the key people I wanted to interview was Rob Coleman, who played a huge role in the early days of the show, and directed two of the best episodes from the first season: "Downfall of a Droid" and "Duel of the Droids."

As with many interviews, our phone chat lasted considerably longer than the finished piece. For a start, Coleman was so enthusiastic about his work that one question set him off for a considerable time—an interviewer's dream!

At the end of the interview, I asked if we could speak again to discuss *Star Wars: The Phantom Menace* as it was due to celebrate its 10th anniversary soon. He took a lot of convincing that it had really been a decade since the movie was released—in fact it had been a good couple of years more when you consider how early on he started working on it.

One thing that the team at *Insider* never takes for granted is the generosity of cast and crew members who take the time to speak with myself or the other writers of the magazine. It's unpaid, and costs time for people who are often very busy with successful careers. It's always hugely appreciated, and there would be no *Star Wars Insider* without them.**—Jonathan Wilkins**

Rob Coleman was born April 27, 1964, in Canada. He spent 14 years working for Lucasfilm at Industrial Light & Magic and Lucasfilm Animation. He worked very closely with George Lucas on the Star Wars *prequels. He featured on* Entertainment Weekly's *'It List' in 2002 as their 'It CG-Creature Crafter' for his work on the digital Yoda. Coleman has been nominated twice for an Oscar for his animation work on* Star Wars: The Phantom Menace *and* Star Wars: Attack of the Clones. *He has also been nominated for two BAFTA Awards for* Men in Black *and* Star Wars: The Phantom Menace.

Most recently, Coleman served as the Head of Animation on The LEGO Movie. *He is currently working on both* LEGO Batman *and* Ninjago.

CREATING

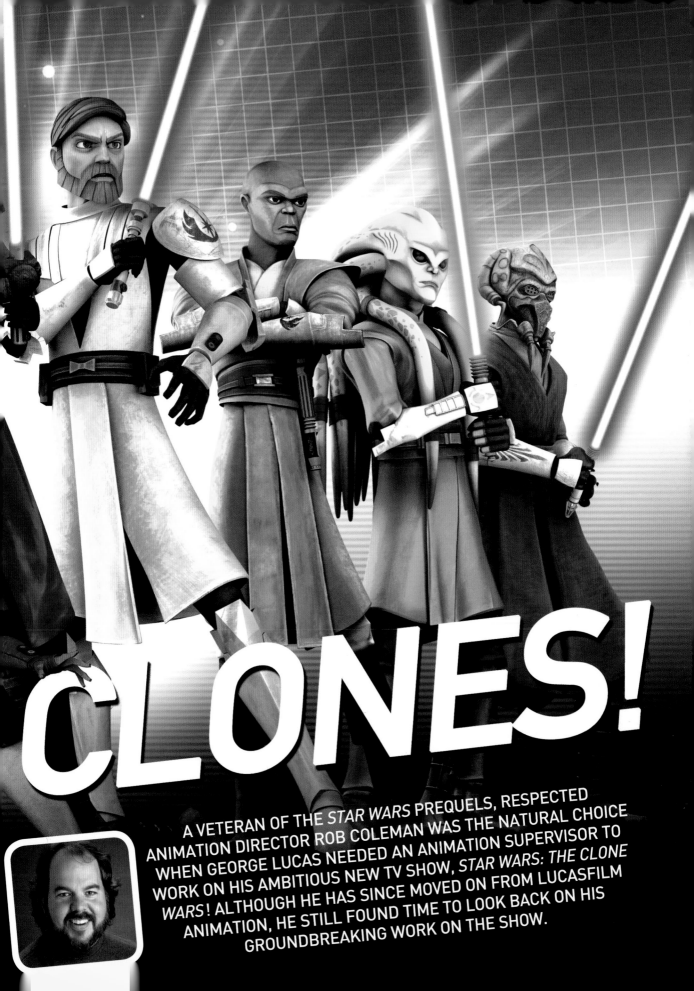

CLONES!

A VETERAN OF THE *STAR WARS* PREQUELS, RESPECTED ANIMATION DIRECTOR ROB COLEMAN WAS THE NATURAL CHOICE WHEN GEORGE LUCAS NEEDED AN ANIMATION SUPERVISOR TO WORK ON HIS AMBITIOUS NEW TV SHOW, *STAR WARS: THE CLONE WARS*! ALTHOUGH HE HAS SINCE MOVED ON FROM LUCASFILM ANIMATION, HE STILL FOUND TIME TO LOOK BACK ON HIS GROUNDBREAKING WORK ON THE SHOW.

When did you first get involved in *Star Wars: The Clone Wars*?

I worked very closely with George Lucas on the prequel films and we had conversations about setting up an animation division while we were shooting *Revenge of the Sith*. That was around 2003.

I didn't officially become involved until I completed all the animation on *Revenge of the Sith*. I started talking to Gail Currey, who I'd worked with at ILM [Industrial Light and Magic] and who was putting together Lucasfilm Animation at that point. She and George invited me to come aboard and help set it up. My first job in May 2005 was to fly over to Singapore to hold a presentation to help attract talent in order to build the studio there.

What are the day-to-day challenges of an animation consultant?

Dave Filoni, the series' supervising director, and Catherine Winder, our launch producer, had both worked in animation before but had not worked in the *Star Wars* universe. George Lucas asked me to meet with them and immerse them in the world of *Star Wars*. The role of animation consultant came out of that early working relationship with Dave Filoni.

Dave is a very talented storyboard artist, and he'd come from doing the 2-D animated *Avatar: The Last Airbender*, but he'd not worked in computer graphics before, and

year, 2005, was tough. We were trying to find the right movement for these characters. George talked about a stylized East-meets-West anime influence, but animated for a North American audience. As an animation consultant, I worked very closely with Dave to craft what that ultimately ended up being the look.

Was *Thunderbirds* ever an influence?

I'm a big fan of *Thunderbirds* and I've actually got some Gerry Anderson stuff here in my home studio, but it wasn't really. I think once people started seeing the images they made an instant connection to Anderson's Supermarionation style, but what Dave Filoni and the art directors were doing in the early days was trying to capture a stylized version of Ralph McQuarrie's inspirational concept paintings for the original *Star Wars* trilogy. As we stylized the animation, it became more like Supermarionation with more articulated faces, but it wasn't something that we pinned up on the board [as an idea].

Was it easier to make a fully animated show as opposed to integrating CGI into live action footage?

It wasn't easier, because we were building a studio from scratch in Singapore and teaching a very green, but very talented, group of people who had never worked at this level before.

he'd not worked with *Star Wars* characters. He is a huge *Star Wars* fan, as the world now knows, but we crafted the role of animation consultant so that I would be able to give input, and critique all animation coming in from our overseas studios. The day to day work was to review the animation and give feedback on the performances. I also worked with Dave to find the right balance of time spent on the animation. For me, that first

"I WAS VERY FLUENT IN GEORGE LUCAS, LET'S PUT IT THAT WAY!"

"I WAS ALWAYS COACHING DIRECTORS TO GO AND LOOK AT THE ORIGINAL *STAR WARS* MOVIE!"

I'd helped build the animation teams at ILM for years and it's a long process. Once we had those established, actually doing the movies was easier because I had people who understood what it was to work at that level. Initially, the TV series was harder because not only was I trying to immerse them in the world of *Star Wars*, I was training them on how to actually animate to the level I wanted.

It is easier animating something that exists only in an animated world, because you can control all the physics and how characters move, as opposed to a live-action and animation combination where you have to be true to the physics and the weight of the human characters. When we were working on Yoda fighting or walking, we were always thinking about gravity, and what does his cloth look like, and what does his skin look like? It had to be photo-realistic. On a stylized animation show like *The Clone Wars*, those problems just aren't there.

How did you make sure the show felt like *Star Wars*?
George Lucas remains very involved and he was extremely involved in the early days, working with Dave Filoni, the writers, and the various episodic directors in describing to us what he was looking for. I was always coaching directors to go and look at the original *Star Wars* movie, so they had an idea of the kind of framing and cutting that George likes. What Dave and Henry Gilroy tried to do in the early days was to recapture that 1977 feel, so—and this is the fun part— there was a lot of homework going back and looking at the old movies and really studying them from a stylistic and directing-choice point of view. We looked at camera choices, cutting choices. George uses a certain kind of lens and there is a certain kind of cutting that he does. Once you become well-versed in that, you can

make him very happy. I'd worked side by side with him for so many years that I had an advantage over the other episodic directors. I already knew how to communicate with George. I was very fluent in George Lucas, let's put it that way!

So you knew what to expect?
Yes. But I was also trying to find a balance. This is Dave Filoni's show. Being asked to be the animation consultant and directing some episodes helped to move the series along. I went over and taught classes in Singapore. I ended up doing the "Downfall of a Droid" and "Duel of the Droids" episodes, which were the very first two shows to come out of Singapore. They wanted me to help shepherd them along, which I was happy to do. They are probably the roughest shows that we did, because they were the first two out of the gate. I've directed three more since then and they are much stronger because the team had more experience and more familiarity with the characters and the cameras than they did in those two episodes.

Is there anything you would change about them?
There is so much I would change! The hardest thing to do as a director is to say, "That's good enough." If you don't start approving work, and you don't have a vision of what you want the show to look like, it will never be finished! I think where I was successful with George was that I was always able to step into the river and say, "That's good enough." The river keeps flowing past you, and you'll see better work coming later on, but you have to stick with what you did before. There are certainly shots in those episodes that I would love to have back, but I don't regret it because we had to deliver the show.

The show is animated in about a fifth of the time of a feature film, so we didn't get

> ## "IF YOU DON'T START APPROVING WORK, AND YOU DON'T HAVE A VISION OF WHAT YOU WANT THE SHOW TO LOOK LIKE, IT WILL NEVER BE FINISHED!"

SELECTED CREDITS

Star Wars: Episode III *Revenge of the Sith* (2005) (animation director)

Signs (2002) (animation supervisor)

Star Wars: Episode II *Attack of the Clones* (2002) (animation director)

Star Wars: Episode I *The Phantom Menace* (1999) (animation director)

Men in Black (1997) (animation supervisor)

Dragonheart (1996) (supervising character animator)

Star Trek Generations (1994) (computer effects artist)

The Mask (1994) (computer graphics animator)

Captain Power and the Soldiers of the Future (animation coordinator) (22 episodes, 1987-1988)

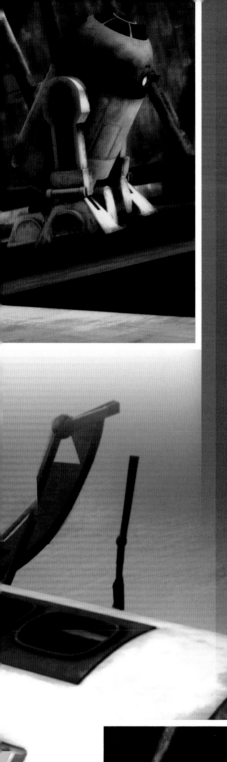

the subtlety and fidelity in the faces and lip-synching in those earlier shows. Later episodes are far better, because I was able to spend time and really hone the team's awareness of what was important in the face. In those earlier episodes it was all hands on deck!

How is an episode put together?

Dave Filoni is the supervising director. He works directly with George Lucas and the writers to create an overall plan for all of the episodes each season. He's there at the beginning with the producer. It usually takes a couple of days to a week, and they plan out in very rough form what will happen.

They come up with episode synopses which are about a paragraph long for each episode, and describe what happens to the heroes, what the problems are, and what gets solved.

The writing team divides up the episodes between them and they start writing. Once the first drafts come in, Dave and George read them and make notes and decisions. Then they start choosing episodes that are actually going to be made. That's when an episodic director gets involved. They'd call the director in and say, "Rob we've got an R2-D2 show coming up"—in my case it was a two parter—"and here's an early draft".

The director gives notes, as a fresh pair of eyes to the story. Then, in maybe a few days or a week, a shooting draft is ready. At that point, the episodic director works with the story-board artists, doing storyboards on paper or computer, or in my case going straight to 3D computer graphics to map out what the scenes are going to look like. You spend maybe six weeks mapping out the whole show, so you have a version of the show done in storyboards

or in computer animatics that describes visually what the show's going to look like.

There might be a still image of Anakin standing, and I would record people in the studio for temp dialogue and work with editor Jason Tucker to cut it all together, so it's to length, but nothing's animated at that stage, and nothing's got color. It's usually just black and white or gray. I'd present that to George, and then he would give me notes. I'd do a revision on that and present it for a final look. Then George would sign off on it.

As an episodic director you "package up the show." This means you make shot-by-shot directing notes on what you want to see happening. You might say Anakin walks onto the bridge of the Twilight. Ahsoka's sitting there with Artoo, and turns to him and says the line. You give director points, like "Anakin's angry at this point because he's just come from such-and-such a place and he's irritated by this or that." When the animators get it in Singapore they understand, because otherwise it could be animated completely out of context. Animators might get five shots in a row, but they may not know what's come before so it's very important as a director that you tell them. Normally, an episodic director would then leave that process and go onto the next show, but I then critiqued, not only the animation coming in for my show, but also for the other four episodic directors.

Were there any examples where it was completely off and they had to start again?

Yes, of course. That was the biggest challenge. It was something I had to get used to. I'd spent 12 years at ILM with my animation crew down the hallway. I could walk into their offices and talk to them at anytime. Now I was in a situation where my animators were on the far side of the Pacific Ocean and I had to wait hours to talk to them because of the time difference! Although

they all spoke English beautifully, there were occasionally communication issues. To be fair, to them, I was used to working with some of the most experienced animators in the world and had a shorthand with them. Now I was dealing with some very talented up-and-coming people, but they didn't have the vocabulary that I was used to. I had to fly over there a few times, and then we got better and better. You'll see as the season goes on, the animation really improves—but that was a learning process for me.

Your episodes feature Ron Perlman as Gha Nachkt—what was he like to work with?
I never got to meet him! Dave Filoni gets all the fun working with the actors. As the supervising director, he directs all the voice talent for all of the shows and it's all done in Los Angeles. I'm holding the fort critiquing all the animation coming in from overseas, and he's down in L.A. meeting Ron Perlman! Dave did get me an autograph though! Ron did a great job in the show. I didn't meet many of the voice talent for *Star Wars*. I never got to meet Andy Secombe, who did the voice of Watto. I never met Brian Blessed who played Boss Nass, so it's not totally out of the norm. I did get to spend so much time with Frank Oz, who played Yoda, that he's become a friend of mine, so that's an added bonus of being the animation director!

What are your favorite scenes from the show?
I really like the writing on those shows, and to be able to see Artoo becoming a tougher little guy was a lot of fun for me. I would say the scene with him fighting with the other droid was a favorite. It was fun to figure out how to shoot that and what was going to happen there. The writers had outlined the entire fight, but as a director you get to pick all the angles, which was fun. The assassin droids coming to life in the hold of the ship was really fun to direct, and to invent how we saw the IG-88s jumping around. We'd only ever seen them standing still in *The Empire Strikes Back*, so to get them to jump and leap and spin their heads around was a highlight for me.

How did you come up with that extreme style of complicated movements?
I was trying to go with the opposite of what the character looked like. If you have a toy or you saw it in the movies, he's just standing there not doing anything. He just looks so rigid, and I thought from an animator's point of view "Let's take that rigidity and just throw it away!" Let's really surprise the fans, so that when these things leap up they're actually much more flexible than their "Tin Man" appearance would allude to. What I was able to do is make it into a vertical fight. I didn't want to just have a fight on the ground; we've seen that so many times. I had this set that had been already outlined in the script where it was described as this big warehouse with shelves upon shelves of droid parts. I went up to the Home Depot store and walked around the aisles. I was thinking,

"Wouldn't it be cool to look up and see those droids jumping and leaping from side to side?" So that's how that started. I thought that was just a neat image.

There's some very creative lighting schemes, such as the sequence where Anakin awakens in the medical bay.
That was harder in the early days when we were doing those droid episodes. Andrew Harris was the Lighting Supervisor for those. All of the color and ideas for the lighting comes through the art department, which Dave Filoni supervises. I can't recall exactly who did the concept paintings for those early shows, but they did some beautiful work. I inherited such beautiful paintings from those guys that I did very few tweaks from a directorial point of view. I really loved what they were doing artistically. The paintings had come with that bleached-out art direction, and I relied heavily on Andrew to pull that off with the Singapore crew.

"I WOULD SAY THE SCENE WITH R2-D2 FIGHTING THE OTHER DROID WAS A FAVORITE!"

"WE USED THE LANGUAGE OF REAL FILM AND APPLIED IT TO THE SHOW."

SPOTTING COLEMAN?

Coleman Trebor, one of the many Jedi slain by Count Dooku in *Attack of the Clones*, is named after Rob Coleman. The man himself has cameos in:

Star Wars: Episode III *Revenge of the Sith* (2005) Opera house patron

Star Wars: Episode I *The Phantom Menace* (1999) Podrace spectator in Jabba's private box

It's quite surprising to see that sort of detail in an animated show.
You've touched on something that was very important to George, Dave, and myself. I keep using the word "shoot" when I talk about making the show because we kept talking about it that way. We thought about it as shooting it with real cameras. This is still an animated world that exists in our imaginations, but we used cinematic tricks that we would use if it were a live-action film. We see lens-flares and exposures as if you're in a dark room and shooting up to a bright window so that everything goes into silhouette. George loves that kind of stuff. So we used the language of real film and applied it to the show.

What kind of scenes do you prefer working on? Big action sequences, like space battles, or smaller, character-based scenes?
I don't actually have a preference. I think every episode or movie has to have a balance. I tended to spend most of my brain power on the quieter character-based scenes, because it was imperative that the animated characters came up to the same level as the real actors. But it was certainly fun to work on the opening space battle in *Revenge of the Sith*.

These TV shows have a lot of action because of the audience we're going for, but it's a real blend. There's a Mace Windu episode that I directed that's coming up later in the season, and that was a real combination of action and character. I'm really proud of that episode. It turns out that they liked it enough to make it the season finale. We were really doing well by the time we got to that show. It's a real blend of big action sequences and smaller character pieces.

I think a strong director is someone who is able to play to people's strengths, because not everybody is good at both of those kinds of scenes. There were specific animators I would give action work to, and other animators I would give acting to, and there's a smaller group who can handle both.

How many episodes did you direct?
I did three more episodes after the two we've talked about. Two of them will be seen in this first season and one of them has been moved to the second season. I'm proud of the droid ones, but there are better ones coming! They do have guest director spots that come up every once in a while, and I would certainly be keen to direct another one. It's all to do with timing and schedule. ☙

THE CLONE WARS
CAST AND CREW

ISSUE 119
JULY/AUGUST 2010

One of the many joys of working on *Star Wars Insider* has been working with the delightful cast and crew of *Star Wars: The Clone Wars*. Headed up by the very talented supervising director, Dave Filoni, the team were all devoted to making the show as great as possible. These efforts paid off marvelously, with a series that broke new ground in both animation and as a drama. As devoted to the craft as they were, the team were equally passionate about the fans. Quite simply, the makers of the show were fans themselves, and established a strong mutual appreciation society with their loyal and extremely appreciative audience. It's certainly true that many of the cast were subscribers to *Insider*.

The team would always be very happy to make themselves available for interview with *Insider*, and always appreciate being featured in the magazine. Tom Kane (Yoda) even uses his cover as a Facebook avatar!
—Jonathan Wilkins

Dave Filoni was the supervising director of Star Wars: The Clone Wars. *Prior to this, he worked on the popular animated series,* Avatar: The Last Airbender. *He is an executive producer on* Star Wars Rebels, *continuing to be a guiding light in* Star Wars *animation.*

Catherine Taber played the part of Padmé in Star Wars: The Clone Wars. *She got her break in the business playing the role of Mission Vao in the classic role-playing game,* Knights of the Old Republic.

Tom Kane took on the daunting role of Yoda in Star Wars: The Clone Wars, *winning acclaim for his performance. He also played the role of the narrator and Wullf Yularen in the series. A much-in-demand actor, Kane has lent his talents to a variety of TV series, videogames, and even voiced Yoda for a TomTom SatNav!*

James Arnold Taylor's performance as Obi-Wan Kenobi in Star Wars: The Clone Wars *includes elements of both Ewan McGregor and Sir Alec Guinness's vocal styles. Taylor also hosts at the* Star Wars Celebration *conventions.*

Matthew Wood's work as a sound designer is rightly acclaimed, but Star Wars *fans probably know him best for the double whammy of providing the voice of General Grievous and the battle droids in* Star Wars: The Clone Wars.

David Acord's career as a sound editor has seen him work on a variety of projects, often collaborating with Matthew Wood. He voiced the GH-7 medical droid in Revenge of the Sith *and will be long remembered for his role as Rotta the Huttlet in the* Star Wars: The Clone Wars *movie.*

Matt Lanter took on the pivotal role of Anakin Skywalker in Star Wars: The Clone Wars, *finding intriguing new depths and angles on the character.*

Sam Witwer's roles in the Star Wars *saga include the mysterious secret apprentice of Darth Vader in the videogame* The Force Unleashed *and the returning villain, Darth Maul, in* Star Wars: The Clone Wars.

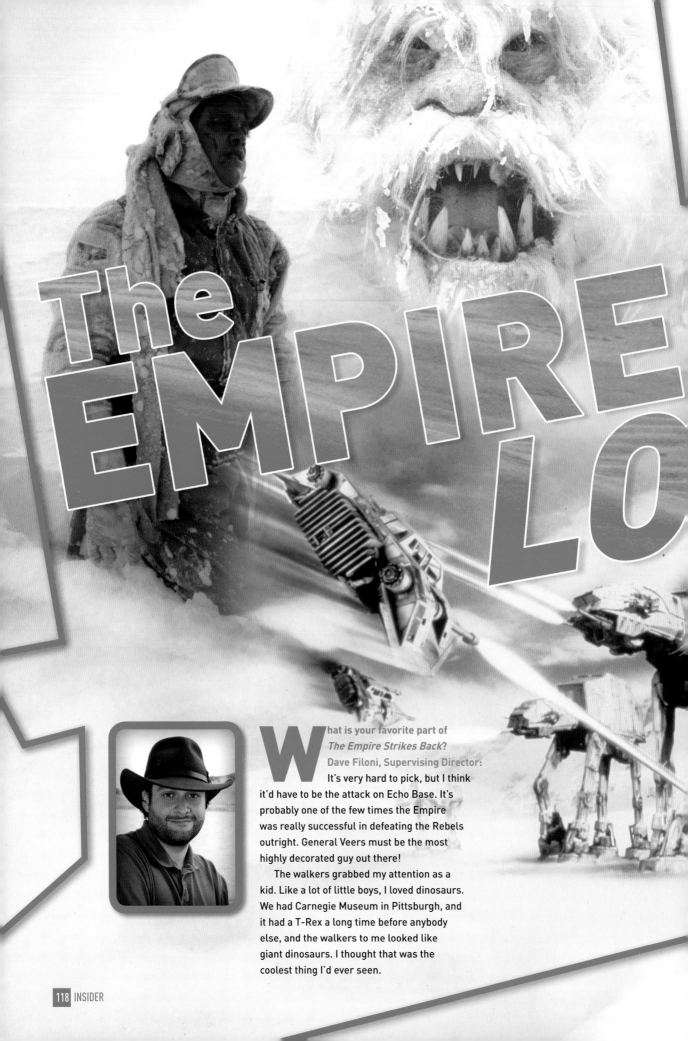

The EMPIRE LO

What is your favorite part of *The Empire Strikes Back*?
Dave Filoni, Supervising Director:
It's very hard to pick, but I think it'd have to be the attack on Echo Base. It's probably one of the few times the Empire was really successful in defeating the Rebels outright. General Veers must be the most highly decorated guy out there!

The walkers grabbed my attention as a kid. Like a lot of little boys, I loved dinosaurs. We had Carnegie Museum in Pittsburgh, and it had a T-Rex a long time before anybody else, and the walkers to me looked like giant dinosaurs. I thought that was the coolest thing I'd ever seen.

OKS BACK

By Pablo Hidalgo

EVERYONE HAS HIS OR HER FAVORITE MOMENTS FROM EPISODE V, AND WE ALL CARRY OUR OWN UNIQUE PERSPECTIVES ON WHAT MAKES *THE EMPIRE STRIKES BACK* SO MEMORABLE. THIS INCLUDES THE TALENTED PEOPLE BEHIND THE CURRENT INCARNATION OF THE ONGOING *STAR WARS* SAGA, *STAR WARS: THE CLONE WARS.*

Catherine Taber, Padmé Amidala: Yoda, the AT-ATs, being scared by the wampa! There's so many. I remember really liking the outfits on Hoth. I have some Hoth-ish boots now because of it.

James Arnold Taylor, Obi-Wan Kenobi: I remember how cool the *Millennium Falcon* was. I remember when they cut the tauntaun open. I was blown away thinking, "*Star Wars* was amazing, but this is beyond anything I have ever seen!" It was the perfect movie experience.

My favorite Han and Leia moment is when they're walking down the hall on Hoth, and he's leaving, and they're having their argument. I love that acting and the reality of that moment within this universe. You don't only see them doing just the cool things in space. It's also the real life stuff that's going on. I love the subtlety of the moment.

Matthew Wood, Supervising Sound Editor, Voice of General Grievous: Seeing *The Empire Strikes Back* when I was eight was one of the first times I can remember feeling the progression of time as a child. Watching the characters we loved from *A New Hope* grow and struggle against adversity in that film made me believe those characters had been out there for the last three years fighting the Empire. No other movie sequel has ever come close to the technical achievements, dramatic story, and overall excitement that *Empire* had.

Tom Kane, Yoda: One of my clearest memories was the dramatic difference in the way the audience was acting. I saw *Star Wars* opening night in 1977, and no one had any idea what they were in for. That audience was a typical "talking quietly, munching popcorn, sipping soda" group. But not at the opening night of *Empire*! That night the theater was electrified. People were in costume, battling in the aisles with their homemade lightsabers, talking about *nothing* but *Star Wars*. After the previews, when the theater went dark... well, the roar of the crowd rivaled any THX sound effect in the movie!

Matt Lanter, Anakin Skywalker: There are so many memorable things from *Empire*, but I guess what sticks out is just the image of the blinding white ice planet of Hoth. It just really set the tone of the Rebels hiding away from the Empire.

David Acord, Sound Designer: There are loads of great moments in *Empire*, but one that sticks out the most to me is probably the climactic lightsaber duel between Luke and Vader. The misty, contrasting blue and orange lighting and the eerie ambient sounds made the carbon-freezing chamber such a creepy environment. Vader was so frightening in those scenes because he was so calculating and so relentless.

If you could take on the vocal role of anyone in *Empire*, who would it be?

Lanter: Well, I'm a *huge* Han Solo fan.

Taylor: I think I'd be the tauntaun. No, honestly, I would have loved doing the Emperor. It was before we really knew him. I loved that character because there was so much mystery behind him.

Wood: Well, aside from my stellar performance as a Rebel pilot in the snowspeeder launch sequence who yells "Mount the tow cable!" [audible in the 2004 DVD version of *Empire*], to play Yoda, loved, I would have.

Acord: Darth Vader. There is no way I could fill James Earl Jones' shoes, but that character is all about the vocal performance.

Tom, what advice would Admiral Yularen have given to the ill-fated Imperial officers that served under Darth Vader?

Kane: To remember that even though their *government* has turned to the dark side, it doesn't mean that *they* have to. That it is their duty to do what they can to protect the citizens as much as possible from the evil of the Empire. I would like to think Yularen and many of the other senior officers who served loyally in the Republic were perhaps working behind the scenes to thwart Vader and the Emperor. Maybe that's why so many admirals made so many serious "mistakes." Those "mistakes" almost always led to their deaths when Vader found out, but they did slow down Vader's plans, didn't they?

Do you look at Vader differently in *Empire* now that you've gotten to know Anakin so well in *The Clone Wars*?

Lanter: Yes, I think so. I see him with more compassion, and hopefully that's what *The Clone Wars* is doing for this *Star Wars* audience. His fall is so much more tragic now that we know he was actually a good guy once.

Taylor: I look at all the characters differently thanks to the prequels and *The Clone Wars*. I look at Vader now not just as this faceless, dark bad guy. I look at him as all of us. I think he is a great example of who we all are as people in that we constantly try to do the right thing, but our emotions and our lives get in the way of reality, and we stop looking at the truth and look to ourselves to try and fix things. ☻

From a sound design point of view, what stands out the most from *Empire*?

Acord: From the ambiances, to the effects to the score, *Empire* is heavy. You can feel the weight in every scene. It's very intense.

Wood: I loved the carbon-freezing chamber ambiance. During one of my first jobs at Skywalker Sound, I put up the original 1/4" reels of the sound effects Ben Burtt designed for those scenes, closed my eyes and felt like I was there. I also love the snowspeeder and AT-AT battle on Hoth. There were a few moments in that film where the audio track was only driven by the sound effects, and they hold up as well as the John Williams score.

Cat, do you think Padmé would have been charmed by Lando Calrissian?

Taber: I think she would have been charmed initially, but once he betrayed them, I'm pretty sure she would have punched him in the face!

BORIS 80

FEATURING GUEST EDITOR WARWICK DAVIS!

STAR WARS
INSIDER ®

CELEBRATING 30 YEARS OF RETURN OF THE JEDI

With
**MARK HAMILL
ANTHONY DANIELS
AND MORE**

TITAN
ISSUE 143
AUG/SEPT
2013
Display until
Sept 03 2012
U.S. $7.99
CAN $9.99

43 >

0 74808 01805 5

PLUS: EXCLUSIVE FICTION! ✦ **ALL-NEW COLLECTIBLES!** ✦ **RARE PHOTOS!** ✦ **EWOKS!**

WARWICK DAVIS
WICKET THE EWOK

ISSUE 143
AUGUST/SEPTEMBER 2013

Warwick Davis was the first actor to be cast in a *Star Wars* film who grew up being a fan of the films, so it's no surprise that he is so popular with *Star Wars* fans.

Witty, self-deprecating, and above all kind and very generous with his time, at the time of featuring Warwick as guest editor of *Star Wars Insider*, he was enjoying a spectacular run of success, featuring in numerous television shows, on stage, and at conventions, often as a stage host. He'd just had a hit sitcom with Ricky Gervais, which poked fun at his persona. The show portrayed him as a greedy, desperate, and often bitter man. This is the complete opposite of the man himself, who generously came to the office, spent an afternoon with us taking photos, being interviewed, and suggesting ideas for the magazine which was created to celebrate 30 years since the release of what was, at that point, the final *Star Wars* movie. How little we knew!

Such is Warwick's professionalism and kindness that he was even happy to sign autographs for staff members who had learned he was coming to visit.

Warwick contributed to a number of features in this issue, but I think the best was his acting masterclass. I like to think that the new cast-members embarking on their roles in the new wave of movies will take some of his invaluable advice!—**Jonathan Wilkins**

Born in Epsom, in southern England, on February 3, 1970, **Warwick Ashley Davis** *was born with Spondyloepiphyseal dysplasia congenita, a very rare form of dwarfism. When he was 11, his grandmother responded to a radio advert calling for people who were 1.2 meters tall or shorter to appear in the forthcoming* Star Wars *film,* Return of the Jedi. *Davis, a fan of the films, applied, and ended up replacing a temporarily ill Kenny Baker as Wicket, the young Ewok who befriends Princess Leia and the rebels. The part led to a busy career including two spin-off Ewok movies, a starring role in the 1988 Lucasfilm blockbuster,* Willow, *and a comedy series,* Life's Too Short, *with Ricky Gervais and Stephen Merchant.*

WARWICK DAVIS PRESENTS
A *STAR WARS*
ACTING MASTER

With *Star Wars* Episode VII on the way, actors everywhere
are keen to have a part in the new movie. Here's what I've
learned about acting in the *Star Wars* films!

CLASS

LEARN YOUR TECHNICAL JARGON CAREFULLY!

It's all about talking nonsense, but making it sound important and valid when you're talking about weaponry or transporting yourself.

A lot of actors on *A New Hope* had trouble saying their lines because they really didn't mean anything. It's easy to look back at the films, because they have validated everything by saying it the way they did, so it now sounds like something real. But if you pick up that script for the first time and look at it, it's absolute nonsense!

It's similar to when I did an episode of *Doctor Who* recently. Some of the dialogue was really hard to say. It makes sense within the story, but it's not how you'd normally speak. You've got to try and give validity to nonsense.

Warwick uses his imagination to work with Watto—a digital character who was added later during Episode I's postproduction.

IMAGINATION WHEN WORKING WITH GREENSCREEN

Make sure you can tap into your childhood imagination. If you want to be an actor in *Star Wars*, you've got to be able to grab hold of the imagination and get it working, particularly in films in recent times where they didn't build any of the sets! They just stick you in front of a greenscreen and say, "Right, this is what's happening!" You have to imagine the environment, the creatures or the beings that are there with you. You even have to imagine holding props that don't exist!

One particular scene I had to do in Episode I comes to mind. I was given the direction, "Grab hold of an eopie and pull its reins. It doesn't want to come with you at first, it's a bit resistant, and you have to tug on it, and then struggle with it walking out of the scene." I said, "Okay, so there'll be some reins hanging off a green pole or something?" But there weren't. I had to imagine the whole scenario.

You're responsible for selling the effect to the audience, because ILM could come in and create something brilliant visually. But if the actors don't believe, the effect won't look real. It's as much about the actor as what ILM puts in there.

EXPECT TO PLAY A CHARACTER BEGINNING WITH "W" (IF YOU'RE ME)

Wicket, Willow, Wald, and Weazel! Nearly all my Lucasfilm characters have names beginning with the letter "W."

I might come up with a bad, dark side villain name beginning with 'W' to see if I can get a part in the new *Star Wars* film! I don't know how to turn this into an acting tip, other than come up with a name beginning with "W" and you'll end up in *Star Wars* (if you're me)!

NEVER EAT OR DRINK PROPS!

It was my first day on the Episode I shoot. I was dressed as Weazel and we were sitting in a grandstand watching the Podrace. Watto was next to me and they had two extremely bright lights to simulate the Tatooine suns. We imagined the Podracers going left to right, and they blew fans at us to show the exhaust draught of the vehicles, and we'd have to react.

A lady would come round serving chips and *Star Wars* juice. It wasn't your regular juice, it was six different types of juice mixed together, so it was a very unpleasant color and tasted very odd. I had some of that and took some of these chips, which had been dyed with food coloring and looked just as odd. So I'd watch the podracer go by, have a drink and eat the crisps—terrific!

We did it from various angles throughout the morning and I had to match my actions and keep sipping the drink, eating the chips, and so on. With the bright lights shining on me, I began to feel pretty ill. I had a horrible stomach ache, indigestion, and a headache. So I laid back in-between takes and fell asleep. Then I felt a tapping on my foot and George Lucas had come over. He said "Hey, Warwick! Glad to have you back onboard." I'd been fast asleep; it was very embarrassing. I'd been going on about being in this film and on my first day, I fall asleep. It's so unprofessional. I didn't explain I had indigestion; I just said, "Oh, yes, sorry." It's pride, isn't it?

Mark Hamill took notice of that, didn't he? In *A New Hope* he doesn't actually eat any of Aunt Beru's food. He moves it around his plate a bit. There's a lesson to be learned there, I think. I bet he never nodded off on set with tummy ache!

ANYBODY CAN ASK FOR YOU TO BE "FASTER, MORE INTENSE"

Rick McCallum [*Star Wars* prequel trilogy producer] was directing the scene at the end of *The Phantom Menace*, where the Jedi Council members come off the shuttle with Chancellor Palpatine. I was there playing Yoda. There was a lot of greenscreen involved, but there was a ramp coming off the ship, as they built part of the set at Leavesden. Rick said, "Come down the ramp and make your way down to Ian [McDiarmid]." I heard, "Action!" and started coming down the ramp, doing the thing with the stick and making the Yoda noise, because you can't help it.

I heard, "Cut!" I don't think I'd even got to the bottom of the ramp. Rick said, "Hey, Warwick, we need you to get over here a bit quicker."

I did it again, and he called, "Cut!" He said, "Warwick, we've got to get you down quicker." I said, "I'm Yoda, Rick. He doesn't move quickly, does he?" Obviously, we hadn't seen Episode II by then, so I didn't know he could leap around. I did try, but there was only so much I could do or he wasn't Yoda anymore in my eyes. I could have jogged over there, but it would have looked ridiculous. I couldn't be faster. but I could be more intense!

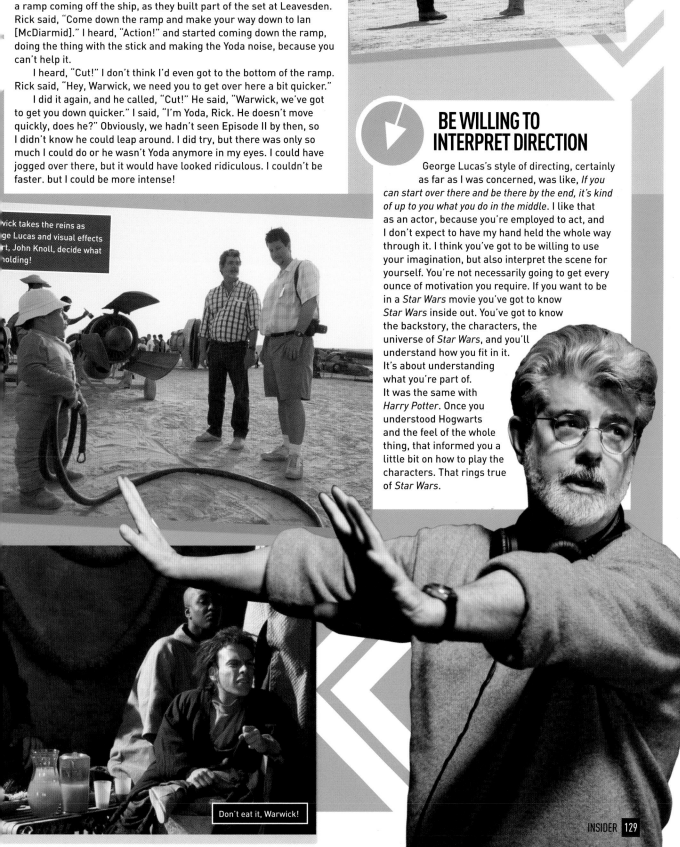

Producer Rick McCallum asks Warwick to speed things up... in an intense style!

...vick takes the reins as ...ge Lucas and visual effects ...t, John Knoll, decide what ...olding!

Don't eat it, Warwick!

BE WILLING TO INTERPRET DIRECTION

George Lucas's style of directing, certainly as far as I was concerned, was like, *If you can start over there and be there by the end, it's kind of up to you what you do in the middle.* I like that as an actor, because you're employed to act, and I don't expect to have my hand held the whole way through it. I think you've got to be willing to use your imagination, but also interpret the scene for yourself. You're not necessarily going to get every ounce of motivation you require. If you want to be in a *Star Wars* movie you've got to know *Star Wars* inside out. You've got to know the backstory, the characters, the universe of *Star Wars*, and you'll understand how you fit in it. It's about understanding what you're part of. It was the same with *Harry Potter*. Once you understood Hogwarts and the feel of the whole thing, that informed you a little bit on how to play the characters. That rings true of *Star Wars*.

MAKE A MINI-MOVIE PRIOR TO YOUR FIRST APPEARANCE

Capitalize on the moment! You're in *Star Wars*, so shoot a movie about how you got the part and tie it in to *Star Wars*. That's much easier these days. Everyone can shoot a movie on their phone, although if you get caught you will be kicked off the film, so there are two sides to this. Take advantage of it, but then don't get caught doing it.

Right: Scenes from *Return of the Ewok*! **Below:** The many faces of Warwick Davis, including Wald and Grimey from Episode I!

EXPECT YOUR CHARACTER TO HAVE NO BACKSTORY... UNTIL THE EXPANDED UNIVERSE CREATES IT

Star Wars does leave you with a lot of questions about the characters. There a lot of characters in there where we only find out about them in the books and the Expanded Universe beyond that. Even as far as reading the back of an action-figure packet, you think, *Ah, that's where he started or that's what it's all about.* That can leave some actors quite frustrated. Some work on their backstory and want to know everything about their character since the day they were born, but with *Star Wars* you won't get that. You'll only get that after you've done it. When it's too late.

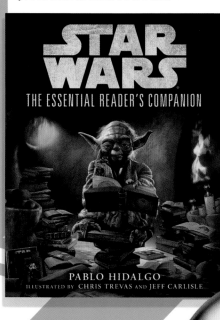

STAR WARS
THE ESSENTIAL READER'S COMPANION

PABLO HIDALGO

ILLUSTRATED BY CHRIS TREVAS AND JEFF CARLISLE

DON'T JUST PLAY ONE CHARACTER

If you've got a day off on a *Star Wars* film, don't go swanning around at the hotel thinking, *This is great! I'm earning money, but I'm not having to work.* Get yourself down to the set, get in the wardrobe tent, and grab various bits of other people's costumes, put them on and get on the set. They will put you in the scene. Then you'll be in it as someone else who initially won't have a name, but if you have a word with George and come up with something beginning with "W," you'll then have a name as well. From there, you'll probably get a trading card, an action figure, and it'll be another one to sign at conventions!

DON'T ASK CRAZY QUESTIONS!

There was a question that had stumped me ever since I first saw *Star Wars*. When Luke and Han put the stormtrooper costumes on, I thought, *Hang on a minute! How have they put them on? I thought they were robots in there, like androids*. I asked George Lucas this question—I can't remember when. I'm hoping it was on *Jedi* and not when we were doing *Willow* when I was 17. I said, "What's with the stormtrooper thing? Is it a man in there or is it a robot?" And he said, "It's a man. The stormtroopers are clones."

Warwick and Carrie Fisher have fun on the set of *Return of the Jedi*. **Below, right:** If only Warwick had seen this picture earlier! Fame at last, as Wicket makes it onto Topps bubblegum card packaging!

KEEP SECRETS!

I've got very few photos of Episode I, but I've got loads of *Jedi* because, by the time it got to Episode I, it was locked down and secret. *Jedi* was called *Blue Harvest* to keep it a secret, but we were all allowed to take pictures, because there was no Internet. Nowadays you take a picture and it can go around the world within seconds. You have to sign your life away to say you will not talk about the film or take photos. So I have very few photos on set in Tunisia, maybe three or four. When I was nervous I took them from under my cape.

When you're an actor, it's very much like being a *Mission: Impossible* spy where you're not allowed to say what your job is, or what you're doing. And you can't even say it to your family because they've all got Facebook or Twitter accounts! You've got to be very careful what you say until the mission is over, and then you can talk about it, at which point nobody is interested. It's old news by then!

Topps

STAR WARS
RETURN OF THE JEDI

10 CARDS • 1 STICKER
1 STICK BUBBLE GUM

Say hi to Warwick and keep up-to-date with him on Twitter at @WarwickADavis

HARRISON FORD ON BECOMING HAN SOLO!

ANGRY BIRDS STAR WARS TAKE FLIGHT INSIDE!

STAR WARS
INSIDER

EXCLUSIVE INTERVIEW!
GEORGE LUCAS
KATHLEEN KENNEDY
ON THE FUTURE OF *STAR WARS*

PLUS!
BOBA FETT
TIMOTHY ZAHN
CELEBRATION VI

TITAN

ISSUE 138
U.S. $7.99
CAN $9.99

JAN/FEB 2013
Please display
until 1/28/2013

0 74808 01805 5

HARRISON FORD
HAN SOLO

From day one, Harrison Ford has epitomized the idea of the reluctant star. Often cagey in interviews, Ford prefers to let his work speak for itself. And, as this interview shows, it wasn't the sudden leap into superstardom that set that agenda.

This interview, from the treasure trove supplied by *Star Wars* publicist Charles Lippincott, captures Ford in a somewhat dry mood. While the actor had appeared in many films previously (he made his movie debut about 10 years before in a James Coburn movie entitled *Dead Heat on a Merry-Go-Round*) it was *American Graffiti* that established him as a screen presence before *Star Wars* propelled him into the light.

Of particular note in the interview is that, amongst the images, there is a shot of Ford assisting with the audition process. The girl auditioning for Leia, Terri Nunn, would not get the part, but would find brief fame in the mid-1980s as the lead singer with the pop group Berlin, who scored a huge international hit with their song, "Take My Breath Away" from the movie *Top Gun*.—Jonathan Wilkins

Harrison Ford was born July 13, 1942. His mother, Dorothy, was a homemaker and former radio actress, and his father, Christopher Ford, was an advertising executive and a former actor. His brother, Terence, was born in 1945.

An active member of the Boy Scouts of America, he achieved its second-highest rank, Life Scout, and worked as a counselor for the Reptile Study merit badge (ironic, given Indiana Jones's notable phobia of snakes). In 1960, Ford graduated from Maine East High School in Illinois. He later attended Ripon College in Wisconsin. It was there that he began attending drama classes in his senior year to get over his shyness, and began to act.

ISSUE 138
JANUARY/FEBRUARY 2013

THIS MONTH, FAR, FAR AWAY....

The Clone Wars: Darth Maul: Shadow Conspiracy released

Scoundrels released

Star Wars: Purge: The Tyrant's Fist, Part 2 released

The Clone Wars: "Missing in Action" aired

Star Wars 1: In the Shadow of Yavin, Part One released

The Clone Wars: "Point of No Return" aired

The Clone Wars: "Eminence" aired

J.J. Abrams is announced as the director for *Star Wars: Episode VII The Force Awakens*

The Clone Wars: "Shades of Reason" aired

Fate of the Jedi: Apocalypse paperback released

Star Wars: Agent of the Empire— Hard Targets, Part 4 released

Angry Birds Star Wars Sticker & Poster Activity Annual 2013 released

Angry Birds Star Wars Super Doodle Activity Annual 2013 released

The Clone Wars: "The Lawless" aired

Star Wars: Blood Ties: Boba Fett Is Dead paperback released

Star Wars: Dark Times 23: Fire Carrier, Part 1 released

Makeup artist Stuart Freeborn dies at 98

The Clone Wars: "Sabotage" aired

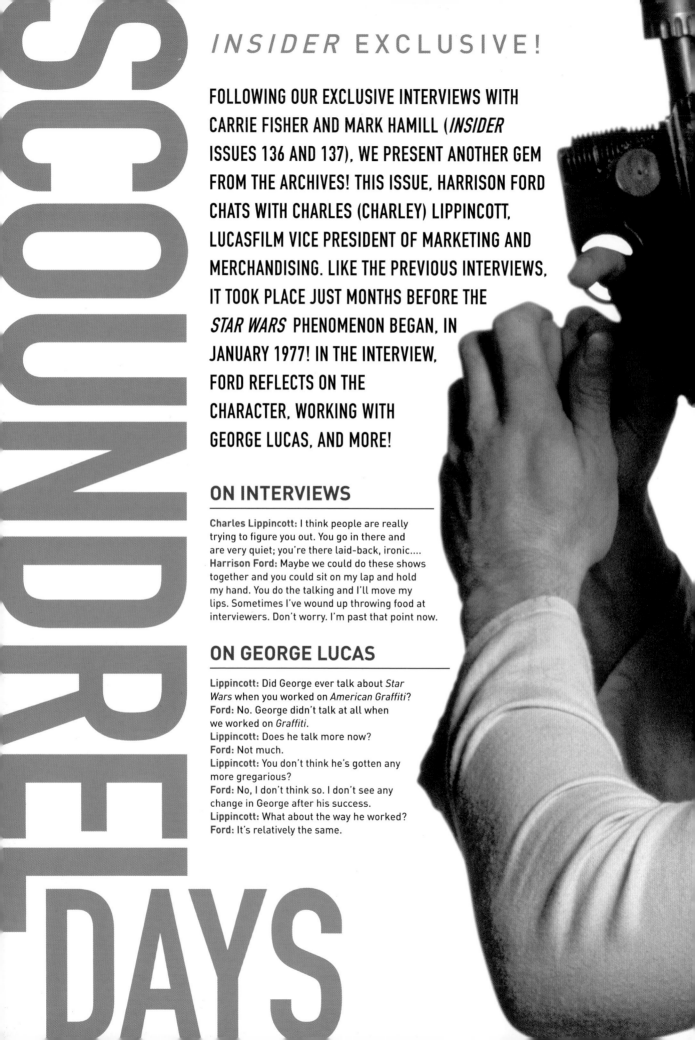

SCOUNDREL DAYS

FOLLOWING OUR EXCLUSIVE INTERVIEWS WITH CARRIE FISHER AND MARK HAMILL (*INSIDER* ISSUES 136 AND 137), WE PRESENT ANOTHER GEM FROM THE ARCHIVES! THIS ISSUE, HARRISON FORD CHATS WITH CHARLES (CHARLEY) LIPPINCOTT, LUCASFILM VICE PRESIDENT OF MARKETING AND MERCHANDISING. LIKE THE PREVIOUS INTERVIEWS, IT TOOK PLACE JUST MONTHS BEFORE THE *STAR WARS* PHENOMENON BEGAN, IN JANUARY 1977! IN THE INTERVIEW, FORD REFLECTS ON THE CHARACTER, WORKING WITH GEORGE LUCAS, AND MORE!

ON INTERVIEWS

Charles Lippincott: I think people are really trying to figure you out. You go in there and are very quiet; you're there laid-back, ironic....
Harrison Ford: Maybe we could do these shows together and you could sit on my lap and hold my hand. You do the talking and I'll move my lips. Sometimes I've wound up throwing food at interviewers. Don't worry. I'm past that point now.

ON GEORGE LUCAS

Lippincott: Did George ever talk about *Star Wars* when you worked on *American Graffiti*?
Ford: No. George didn't talk at all when we worked on *Graffiti*.
Lippincott: Does he talk more now?
Ford: Not much.
Lippincott: You don't think he's gotten any more gregarious?
Ford: No, I don't think so. I don't see any change in George after his success.
Lippincott: What about the way he worked?
Ford: It's relatively the same.

HAN AND LEIA

Ford: The Princess is the product of that world, and has her own intelligence and wit. There's no doubt about it that it's the same for all of us. It's built in. A certain amount of your behavior is based on accepting your environment and a certain amount is based on a resistance to those things you want to change. Her cynicism about her environment is what makes her the right kind of Princess for the movie.

Main image, right: Harrison Ford as Han Solo takes control.

Left, top: A publicity shot for *The Empire Strikes Back*, with Chewie (Peter Mayhew), C-3PO (Anthony Daniels), and R2-D2 (Kenny Baker).

Middle: Auditioning with Terri Nunn (later to find fame with the pop group, Berlin). Note the back of George Lucas' head on the right of shot.

Bottom: The cast of *A New Hope* pause for breath on the Death Star.

Below: Harrison Ford and Mark Hamill relax between shots.

ON AUDITIONING

Lippincott: Did George interview actors for *Graffiti* like he did for *Star Wars*?
Ford: As I remember, the interviews for *Graffiti* were just normal interviews conducted by Fred Roos, and then there were videotape tests.
Lippincott: Diane Crittendon [*Star Wars* casting director] asked you to audition for the role. Is that right?
Ford: No, I think Fred Roos insisted about three weeks before production started. George had let out the word beforehand to the *Graffiti* people that he wasn't going to use anybody from *Graffiti*.
Lippincott: Did you test with Jodie Foster?
Ford: I really don't remember. I do remember Robby Benson.
Lippincott: You read with Mark Hamill. Mark told me that.
Ford: Yeah, well, I don't remember it very well.
Lippincott: Did George ever talk about the fact that he thought you'd be Han Solo?
Ford: No.
Lippincott: He never did?
Ford: No.
Lippincott: Never brought it up?
Ford: No. It would come to me in other ways.
Lippincott: Had he talked about the character before you first did the scene?
Ford: No. Not much. Fred insisted that it was an extension of Bob Falfa [Ford's character in *American Graffiti*]. Which I thought was wrong.
Lippincott: Did you have an image in mind for the character?
Ford: I thought it was real clear. I don't know how to describe the picture of him that I had in my mind, but I knew from the beginning what he was like.

"I DON'T KNOW HOW TO DESCRIBE THE PICTURE
[OF HAN] I HAD IN MY MIND,
BUT I KNEW FROM THE BEGINNING
WHAT HE WAS LIKE."

ON PRODUCER GARY KURTZ

Ford: Gary Kurtz never really spoke to the actors about anything but business. We only came to know what it was that Gary was doing after a certain period of time when he would show up with stacks and stacks of papers done in 19 different color pencils showing how the shot was to be laid out, stuff like that. Only then did we become aware of what his real competencies were.

ON HAN SOLO

Lippincott: Did you have a total concept of your character?

Ford: No, I didn't have a total concept because I didn't know the other people.

Charley: But in reading the script you must have had a concept of your character?

Ford: Well, I don't make conscious decisions like that. I just read it a couple of times and go in with what seems right and go from there. I'm not particularly aware of the elements of that decision.

Lippincott: I assume it's intuitive to a certain extent.

Ford: It better be, because otherwise there's no excuse for it at all.

Lippincott: There are English actors who get into this whole thing and talk about how they objectively reach that.

Ford: I don't understand.

Lippincott: I do sense that type of training from Carrie.

Ford: Yeah. They break down scenes into who, what, where, that kind of stuff?

Lippincott: So that you can play it without relating yourself to the characters.

Ford: I don't know how to act. It's different every time. It's probably haphazard with me. Until I get locked into something.

> ## "I DON'T KNOW HOW TO ACT SO IT'S DIFFERENT EVERY TIME. IT'S HAPHAZARD WITH ME. UNTIL I GET LOCKED INTO SOMETHING"

TRUST HIM
FOUR FINE FACTS ABOUT FORD

While working as a carpenter, he became a stagehand for the rock band The Doors.

He built a recording studio for Sergio Mendes.

He played the part of Colonel G. Lucas in *Apocalypse Now*.

He has a species of ant and spider named after him—Pheidole harrisonfordi and Calponia harrisonfordi repectively—in honor of his work in conservation.

ON FAME

Lippincott: Do people recognize you?

Ford: No. I mean I'll sit in people's offices and they'll ask me what part I played in *American Graffiti*. And I'll say I was the guy in the cowboy hat. I don't know whether it's that they can't remember the character, but it's obvious that they don't recognize me as that person. The same thing happened with *The Conversation* [Francis Ford Coppola's 1974 movie in which Ford co-starred]. They don't get a fix on it. They can't tell if I'm an indoor or outdoor actor. You know that distinction? You could get called for a Western. Somebody will bring your name up and they'll say, "Nah! He's an indoor actor!"

> "I HAD NO IDEA HOW THEY WERE GOING TO DO SOME OF THE THINGS THAT [WERE IN THE SCRIPT]."

ON WORKING IN ENGLAND

Lippincott: How was it working with the English crew? Was it any different from American crews?

Ford: Beer breaks and stuff. I didn't notice any difference, basically. The English crews are real democratic. I mean, they don't seem to be as "star oriented" as American crews can sometimes be. They treat everybody just about the same and are really pleasant. I don't think that they understood what was going on for a long time. They didn't know what it was that we were acting in and why. They didn't know whether it was some kind of comic book or what. They had no way of knowing that it was operating on several levels at the same time, because it's such an American kind of tale. I think it was the humor they didn't quite see.

Main image, left: Han Solo fighting his way out of trouble aboard the Death Star.

Left: Posing for a publicity shot in the lush redwood forest (*Return of the Jedi*).

Below: A humorous moment from *The Empire Strikes Back*

Bottom: Han Solo and his best pal, Chewbacca!

ON HUMOR IN *STAR WARS*

Ford: There are laughs in *Star Wars*. I don't think there are jokes.

Lippincott: Are you talking about jokes being physical jokes? The jokes are sort of in that long chase through the Death Star.

Ford: There are lots of physical jokes in there.

Lippincott: It may not be apparent when filming.

Ford: Reading that script, I think it was really hard to tell what was coming off. I knew what I thought my character was going to be, but I didn't know what it was going to look like. I had no idea how they were going to do some of the things that were in there, at all. No idea. It was a mystery. And still is to this day.

ON NOT KNOWING WHAT TO EXPECT

Lippincott: Do you think that because you never had an interest in science fiction before, you had no idea how the film would look?

Ford: No, I knew what it was going to kind of look like, but I didn't know how close they were going to come to it, or stylistically how they were going to approach it. I suspected what the style of the film was going to be, and the style of acting that would be called for. But I didn't know what the reality level was going to be. I thought of it as any old road movie. I was one of these people who advances the story. This is the thematic function. I isolated the thematic function of the character easily. It's not as easy to do it in other movies as it was in this picture and that's what I knew I had to do. It was how the character served the story. ☀

STAR WARS

AMAZING NEW
FICTION

RALPH
MCQUARRIE
REMEMBERED

ISSUE 134
JULY 2012
U.S. $7.99 Can $9.99
Display Until 7/24/12

TITAN

STAR THE CLONE WARS

SEASON 5 EXCLUSIVE!

Episode titles revealed! New details teased!

10 GREAT MOMENTS FROM SEASON 4

NILO RODIS-JAMERO
VISUAL EFFECTS

ISSUE 134
JULY 2012

There are certain people who retain an aura of mystery. Nilo Rodis-Jamero is certainly one. A familiar name to fans thanks to his work on *The Empire Strikes Back* and *Raiders of the Lost Ark*, he's not somebody who has often been interviewed.

His work can be seen in many icons of the saga as well as Leia's famous gold bikini and the Imperial biker scout armor.

He insists that he got the job on *Empire* by answering in the negative to all three of George Lucas's questions during his job interview: "Do you like science fiction books? Do you like science fiction movies? Do you like movies?"—**Jonathan Wilkins**

Nilo Rodis-Jamero was born in the Philippines, emigrating to the USA soon after graduating from high school. After graduating from San Jose University, he started his career as a Chevrolet car designer for General Motors. He began working on films after Joe Johnston hired him as a designer for Industrial Light & Magic.

He worked as art director on three of the Star Trek *movies,* Poltergeist, Flubber *and* Home Alone 3. *More recently he served as art director on Tim Burton's blockbusting version of* Alice in Wonderland.

DESIGNS
ON AN
EMPIRE!

ASSISTANT ART DIRECTOR NILO RODIS-JAMERO LIFTS THE LID ON HOW HE GOT HIRED BY GEORGE LUCAS TO HELP CREATE *THE EMPIRE STRIKES BACK.*
INTERVIEW: J. W. RINZLER

Main image:
Slave I and
Boba Fett as
illustrated by
Nilo Rodis-
Jamero (above).

How did you first meet George Lucas before *The Empire Strikes Back*?
I was designing military tanks in San Jose. Within eight months of my one-year contract I was unhappy and was advised to quit. The day my contract ran out, Joe Johnston [special effects art director on the original *Star Wars* trilogy] called me, and said he'd heard about me through San Jose State Industrial Design.

He wanted to know if I was available and invited me to come over for a meeting with George Lucas. I met George in this house that did not have any movie trappings whatsoever. I just thought it was really weird to be interviewed in my suit and tie with my slide projector in somebody else's house.

So there I was with my school portfolio, which was basically a long continuous scroll. To view the scroll, you have to unspool it on the floor. So, while I was

presenting my slide-show, George was on the floor looking at this scroll. He was more interested in my schoolwork than he was with my car designs. At that time I'd just come out from General Motors, designing cars and military tanks, but he was not interested in that at all.

He interrupted my slide presentation three times. He asked, "Do you like science fiction books?" I said, "No." I went on with my presentation, and then he came back up again and said, "Do you like science fiction movies?" I said, "No," and I went on with my presentation. He asked, "Do you like movies?" I said, "No." He said, "Why don't you come and work for me?" I said, "What do you do?" He said, "I make movies." And I said, "Movies are designed?!" I honestly didn't know that! He said, "Have you heard of *THX 1138*?" I said, "No." "Have you heard of *American Graffiti*?" I said, "I heard about that." And he said, "Have you heard of

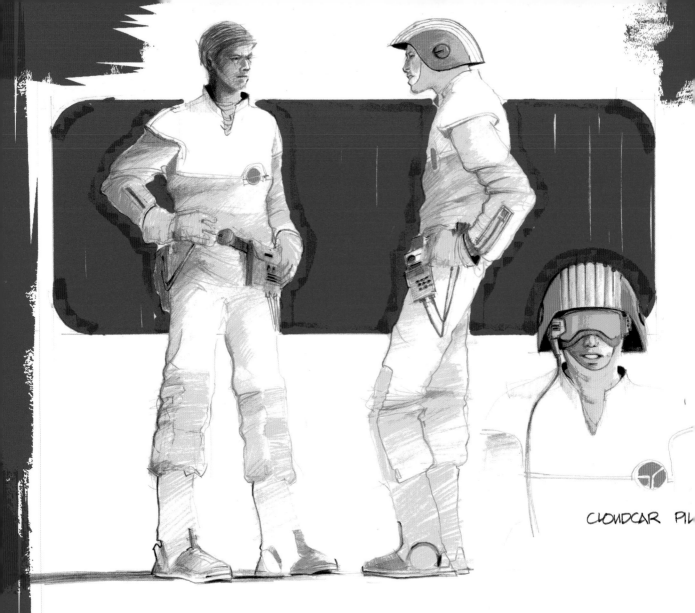

CLOUDCAR PIL

Star Wars?" I said, "I heard that's really good." He said, "I made that!"

Later I asked him, "Why would you hire me? I don't know anything about film." This is almost word-for-word what he said: "You used to do tangible designs. Now I'm asking you to do intangible designs. That's why." I'd never thought of that.

To this day, because of that encounter with George, I tend to hire enthusiastic amateurs instead of seasoned professionals.

What happened next?
Joe never really told me, "Here's how you do it, kid." He'd just say, "Here are some papers and some pens. Tell me what you need."

He took the first floor of the house where we worked [on Ancho Vista in San Anselmo] and I took the second floor, so I'd barely ever see Joe. We would chat but he would leave me alone; then, around noon, we'd get together and have lunch. Then during preproduction, every two weeks or so, George would come in and look at our work.

No specific sequences or characters

were actually given to me. I started seeing Industrial Light & Magic's Phil Tippett and Jon Berg occasionally.

"I ASKED GEORGE LUCAS 'WHAT DO YOU DO?' HE SAID, 'I MAKE MOVIES. HAVE YOU HEARD OF *STAR WARS*? I MADE THAT!"

What was George like to work with?
On *Empire*, I was lining up a shot and George walked in. He was looking at what I was doing, and said, "Do you mind if I move something?" It was the ion cannon shooting into the sky, as the Rebels escape from Hoth. He moved an element that I was framing and said, "Take a look."

All he did was move the foreground gun turret, and the framing suddenly became absolutely brilliant. It was good

design; it was good balance; and in the moment of trying to frame a shot, the designer in me had gotten lost in the minutia of what I was doing.

He always keeps the big picture in mind. George is the painter and I'm merely a brush, and the canvas is his movie. I occasionally have an idea: "You know what would really look good in that sky, George, is the perfect blue." But George takes the brush, and dips you in red paint. I never took offense at the fact that he didn't use my idea, because I was just a tool to his art.

What else do you remember about production on *Empire*?
The first time I met the rest of the crew was after some months of Joe and I working by ourselves. There was really no script that I remember. I was just told to work on sequences or help on sequences through storyboards. I was just framing shots. One day later on, George told us to gather all the storyboards and took us to a bigger room, and in that room

Far left: Concept costume design for the cloud car pilot by Nilo.

Left: An early take on the speeder bikes.

Below: Director Richard Marquand, George Lucas and Nilo work on *Return of the Jedi.*

GOOD ENOUGH!

Nilo Rodis-Jamero: I was hired by Walt Disney Studios to shepherd and produce the special effects for the movie *Flubber* (1997), and I really wanted to hire a New York-based company, called Blue Sky. But Disney had hired me because I had experience working with ILM.

By coincidence, I ran into George. He said, "You know, this is really cool that you're doing this. I'll make you a deal. I'll give you 10 percent off across the board, but you have to make your director accept the first 10 shots." And I said, "That's a no-brainer. I'm going to have Les [Mayfield, the director] accept the first shot. This is the reason why I was hired to begin with—to guide Les—because he had never done a big effects movie before. So I went back to Disney and had a meeting with Les, and he goes, "Absolutely. Ten percent, that's almost like half a million. You know, we can buy a lot of stuff with that." I said, "Great."

The first shot that came in from ILM... Les would not take it. Les would not take the second shot. Les would not take anything, and George came back to me and said, "See." Directors sometimes get so hung up on the first shot, whereas George would always accept the first shot in the belief that it will give you momentum.

And in fact the first few shots don't matter, because what you're really looking for is the momentum and for the technology to catch up somewhere in the 200 shots; then you can come back to the first 10 shots and actually make that even more perfect, but you have to accept them on the first go. It's what in George parlance was "CBB": "could be better," but he accepts it.

On *Empire*, Dennis or Ken would sometimes be saying, "No, no, that's not good enough," and George would just go, "No, that's good enough. Next!"

EAVY AGING THROUGHOUT
LL COLORS VERY SUBDUED

"GEORGE LUCAS IS THE PAINTER AND I'M MERELY HIS BRUSH, AND THE CANVAS IS THE MOVIE."

there was Dennis Muren, Richard Edlund, Ken Ralston, and Phil Tippett.

We didn't have a director at that time. I'm sure George already had Irvin Kershner in mind, but he was not involved in this meeting. Gary Kurtz and Bruce Nicholson [head of the Optical department] were also there. There must have been a boatload of Oscar winners sitting there, but I didn't know.

The opening sequence of *Empire* became mine. George said, "Nilo will explain the first sequence."

Everybody turned to page 14 of the script and Bruce Nicholson raised his hand. George said, "Do you have a problem, Bruce?" Bruce said, "What's the color of the walker?" George looked at me. I didn't say anything. And George goes, "Nilo?" And I said, "White."

We read on to page 40, where the snowspeeders arrive. Bruce again, "What color is the snowspeeder?" And George again goes, "Nilo?" And I go, "White." I wouldn't color it anything other than white.

We got to page 70. George stopped the meeting and said, "Bruce, do you have a problem?" Bruce is still on page 14. He said, "I don't know how to pull a matte of white on white on white on white, because everything

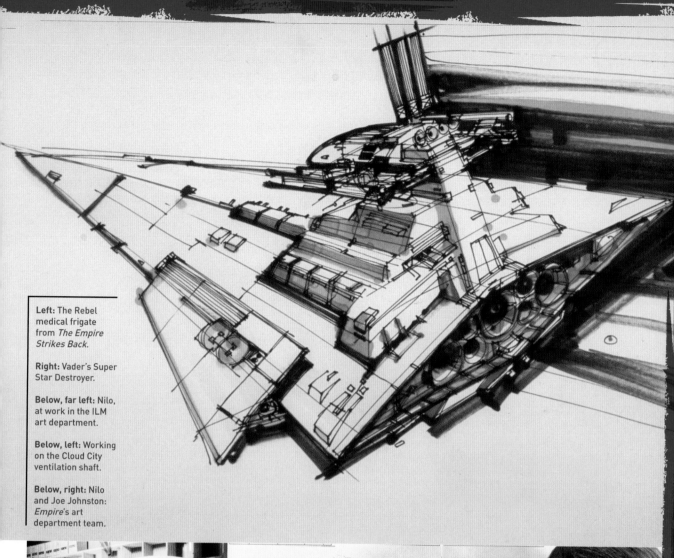

Left: The Rebel medical frigate from *The Empire Strikes Back*.

Right: Vader's Super Star Destroyer.

Below, far left: Nilo, at work in the ILM art department.

Below, left: Working on the Cloud City ventilation shaft.

Below, right: Nilo and Joe Johnston: *Empire*'s art department team.

is in white. The gun turret is white, the Rebel forces are white, the walker is white. Everything is white." George said, "I'm not asking you to pull a matte of white on white on white today. I'm not asking you next week. I may never ask you. Do you want to come and join us on page 70?" Bruce Nicholson later won the Oscar for his work on the movie.

Dennis, Ken, and Richard all embody that sort of thinking. They actually don't have a solution, but they are always able to zoom in on what the problem is. ☺

EXCLUSIVE! WE WANT YOU TO CHOOSE THE NEXT HASBRO ACTION FIGURE!

STAR WARS

A KNIGHT'S TALE!
JAMES ARNOLD TAYLOR, THE VOICE OF OBI-WAN KENOBI, TALKS TO *INSIDER!*

SEA OF CONFLICT!
MEET THE WARRIORS BENEATH THE WAVES

ON THE EDGE!
ROGUES AND SCOUNDRELS REVEALED!

PLUS:
ALL-NEW FICTION BY PAUL S. KEMP

Issue 129
NOV/DEC 2011
U.S. $6.99
CAN $7.99

TITAN

7 25274 01805 5

DENIS LAWSON
WEDGE ANTILLES

ISSUE 129
NOVEMBER/DECEMBER 2011

Denis Lawson rarely talks about his work on *Star Wars*, which is a shame, as Wedge Antilles is a popular character who appears throughout the original trilogy. He even gets to take the shot that helps to destroy the second Death Star during the climactic battle in *Return of the Jedi*!

When this interview was originally published, we received a number of emails and letters—over 50 in fact—thanking us for interviewing him! The cult of Wedge, indeed!—**Jonathan Wilkins**

Denis Lawson *was born in Crieff, Scotland, on September 27, 1947. He was educated at Crieff Primary School (then called Crieff Public School). After the control examination (the Scottish equivalent of the 11 Plus selective admission examination), he went on to Morrison's Academy before attending the Royal Scottish Academy of Music and Drama, having first unsuccessfully auditioned for the Royal Academy of Dramatic Art in London. He then sold carpets and did amateur theater work for a year in Dundee before auditioning again at RADA in London and successfully at RSAMD in Glasgow.*

RED TWO, STANDING BY

AS X-WING PILOT EXTRAORDINAIRE WEDGE ANTILLES, ACTOR DENIS LAWSON HAD A MINOR—BUT NONETHELESS PIVOTAL—PART IN THE *STAR WARS* UNIVERSE. *STAR WARS INSIDER* CAUGHT UP WITH LUKE SKYWALKER'S WINGMAN. INTERVIEW BY CALUM WADDELL

Born in the small town of Crieff, in the picturesque Scottish area of Perthshire, actor Denis Lawson has been one of the U.K.'s most dedicated and prolific thespians for over four decades—appearing on the famously demanding stages of London's West End literally *hundreds* of times (with over 500 performances in the musical *Mr. Cinders* alone). On the screen, Lawson's notable roles include appearances in the classic movie comedy *Local Hero* (1983), the television series *Holby City*, and the acclaimed BBC serial *Bleak House* (2005). However, the actor is also well recognized for playing the role of Wedge Antilles ("Red Two") in all three of the original

Star Wars movies—a part that he would reprise, albeit solely in vocal form, for the 2001 video game *Star Wars* Rogue Squadron II: Rogue Leader (which was released on the Nintendo GameCube).

Notable for surviving the challenge of taking down the dreaded Death Star in *A New Hope*, and returning to X-wing duty in order to tackle some AT-AT action in *The Empire Strikes Back*, Wedge would further prove his worth in *Return of the Jedi*. A fitting filmic farewell for the pilot, the character would successfully aim and fire at the Death Star—finally bringing an end to the rule of the evil Empire.

Lawson, however, admits to being a little bit tongue-tied

"WATCHING *STAR WARS* BEING MADE WAS QUITE SIMILAR TO SEEING AN ENORMOUS ARMY, LUMBERING FORWARD THROUGH THE TRENCHES."

when it comes to things *Star Wars*-related. "I don't really know where to begin when it comes to *Star Wars*," he smiles. "I will say that I think the films are absolutely wonderful entertainment, and I fully understand their popularity, but they did not really have any relevance, or influence, on the rest of my career as an actor. I do not want that to sound disparaging toward the films, however, because I do think that they are excellent and I was happy to be asked back for the sequels—but as an actual acting experience, they were not very exciting."

Certainly, Lawson does concede that this was predominantly due to the fact that the *Star Wars* films were epic productions, and actors with small roles can all too often feel like just another cog in the machinery. "We shot the first one in 1976," he recalls. "I remember speaking to Mark Hamill, who is a really nice man—he was always very easy to chat with and extremely down to earth. But, without wanting to speak for anyone else, I do not think that anybody on the set of the original movie had high expectations of it. I was one of a bunch of young London-based actors who had been hired as part of the supporting cast and we all turned up, unsure of what to expect, to do this huge American movie. It was budgeted at $7 million, which was very big for the time. But considering how small my role was, and how little I had to do, I always felt that my contribution was virtually nothing." Nevertheless, the actor does admit that it was quite a sight to witness the production of *A New Hope* slip into gear.

"Now that was the really interesting aspect of *Star Wars* for me," he enthuses. "Before that, I had never seen a massive movie in the process of being made. If I had to describe it, and it was like this on the sequels too, it was quite similar to an enormous army, lumbering forward through the trenches. The technical aspects of it were utterly fascinating and I really enjoyed watching it happen."

Lawson's *Star Wars* connection continued to the prequels when his nephew, Ewan McGregor, was cast as the young Obi-Wan Kenobi. So did he have any qualms about McGregor taking on a piece of the family tradition?

READERS' CHOICE

Way back in *Star Wars Insider* 38, a readers' poll ranked Wedge Antilles the eighth most popular *Star Wars* character. His high ranking in the poll placed him ahead of popular characters such as Lando Calrissian, Obi-Wan Kenobi, and C-3PO and R2-D2!

"When I heard about Ewan and the *Star Wars* films, I was, at least initially, a little bit apprehensive," says Lawson. "I do think that huge movies like that can drive you into a cul-de-sac as an actor—especially if you have a leading role in them. But, at that point in his career, Ewan had a very strong track record anyway: he had done *Shallow Grave* and *Trainspotting*, which were both big hits, so he was very well established. Thanks to these films, I think people already knew what he was capable of. So, in the end, doing *Star Wars* didn't seem like such a big risk for him. The proof of that is where he is now—Ewan has managed to challenge himself and move onto a career beyond *Star Wars*. He has also done a lot of stuff outside of that genre. He is an excellent actor and he has more than proven that."

Wedge Antilles, on the other hand, remains firmly rooted in the world of *Star Wars*—and his legend has grown since the original trilogy. Indeed, the character has had his background expanded in such book spin-offs as the *Thrawn* trilogy and, most famously, in the comic book series *X-wing: Rogue Squadron*. That news comes as a bit of a surprise to Lawson himself.

"I am shocked to hear that people remember the character, to be honest," he laughs. "I have had *Star Wars* fans come up to me and say, 'Isn't it great that Ewan is in *Star Wars* and you also did those movies? That is really something to be proud of!' But, although I did have fun, as acting roles, they just did not count for a lot. Looking back at my career, I would say that the highlight was *Local Hero*, which I loved, and more recently *Bleak House*. I can definitely tell you that if any of the *Star Wars* fans discover these then I'm happy."

Luke and the first Wedge (Colin Higgins) discuss their chances of surviving to the end of the movie.

> ## "I AM SHOCKED TO HEAR THAT PEOPLE REMEMBER THE CHARACTER, TO BE HONEST."

EXPANDED
Denis Lawson can next be seen alongside Ewan McGregor in the movie *Perfect Sense*.
UNIVERSE

THE THREE WEDGES!
There are actually three actors playing the role of Wedge in *A New Hope*. During the Rebel briefing scene, actor Colin Higgins played the role, but was replaced during the shoot by Denis Lawson. The voice of Wedge was provided by another actor, David Ankrum. Lawson finally used his own voice, some 20 years later, in the videogame *Star Wars: Rogue Squadron II: Rogue Leader*.

Han and Wedge 2, Death Stars 0! The Rebel friends celebrate after taking down another Death Star.

CHEWIE CHAT!
WITH PETER MAYHEW

NEW FICTION! FIRST BLOOD

STAR WARS
INSIDER®

STAR WARS:
THE CLONE WARS

50
GREAT
REASONS TO
REWATCH
SEASON 3!

KATIE
LUCAS
NOTES FROM
THE WRITERS'
ROOM!

CLONE
WARS
EXCLUSIVE

"CLASSIC
CHARACTERS
TO RETURN IN
SEASON 4"
DAVE
FILONI

MEET
THE MAN
WHO BUILT
ECHO
BASE!

Issue 125
MAY/JUNE 2011
US $7.99
CAN $9.99

PETER MAYHEW
CHEWBACCA

ISSUE 125
MAY/JUNE 2011

It's a terrible cliché, but Peter Mayhew is the epitome of the gentle giant. When meeting him in person, it's easy to underestimate just how large he is. Shaking his hand is a humbling experience—you get the feeling that he could crush you in an instant, but he wouldn't; he's Peter, he's Chewbacca. Although sadly he is no longer as steady on his feet as he once was, he is still a warm and witty character to be around.

For a long time, he lived in my hometown, Croydon, a small town just south of London. He could occasionally be seen walking through the local shopping mall, and always, in his wake, were people staring and smiling.

Finally, the opportunity to interview him came thanks to Chewbacca's role in an episode of *Star Wars: The Clone Wars*. Although the show is animated, Peter's distinctive movements were copied to make Chewie more authentic.

The interview here was a phone interview conducted via Lucas Animation's friendly PR lead, named Tracy. Ordinarily, we get a brief period to get the interview done—the shortest being an eight-minute interview that I once conducted at breakneck speed. This generally includes the usual pleasantries, hellos, thank yous, etc. And that usually gets curtailed if the talent is late. In this case I had 30 minutes. We discussed Peter's work on the show and the saga in general.

As the interview came to a close, we ended up talking about Croydon and how it had changed. Peter has been a resident of Texas for a number of years, so was keen to hear what had been going on in his absence.
—**Jonathan Wilkins**

Peter Mayhew (born May 19, 1944) is a British-American actor. Mayhew got his first acting job in 1976 when the producers of Sinbad and the Eye of the Tiger *discovered him from a photograph in a newspaper article about men with large feet, and cast him in the role of the minotaur. When casting his first* Star Wars *film, producer George Lucas needed a tall actor who could fit the role of the hairy alien Chewbacca. He originally had in mind 6 feet 6 inches (1.98 m) bodybuilder David Prowse, but instead Prowse chose to play Darth Vader. This led Lucas on a search, which turned up Mayhew, who says that all he had to do to be cast in the role of Chewbacca was stand up.*

WOOK WORDS!

Can you recall the reaction when you first walked on to the set of *A New Hope* in your full Chewie costume?

Yeah, that would be the Docking Bay 94 set at Elstree Studios in London. There was Harrison Ford (Han Solo) and some extras, and an Irish actor named Declan Mullholland playing Jabba the Hutt, in a scene that didn't make it into the movie. The reaction was that I was just another costume! There was sand all over the place, and it was a question of getting the shots as quickly as possible.

You worked with Alec Guinness on that movie...

Alec was very good. He was a true, true professional. If anything went wrong with his performance, if he screwed up on a line or a look, he'd apologize to everybody and go back and do it again. When he wasn't working, he was a very nice man to sit down and talk to because he had so many fascinatng stories and observations about theater, films, and his long career.

Is it easy to get the Chewie attitude back when you play the role after a long period of time?

It's extremely easy! I don't know what happens, but once the costume is on, I get back into character very easily. It's happened on every shoot that Chewie's been involved with. I arrive on set, put the shoes on, and suddenly Chewie is alive. I don't understand it, but it happens every time I do it.

I did wonder whether it would still happen when I went to Australia to shoot Episode III, but it did. The reaction from the crew was there, so I knew I was doing it right.

For that film, we knew we had to make a new costume because Chewie was younger. However, during the fittings we realized it didn't look right. The problem was that two shoulder

IEE

WITH CHEWBACCA BACK IN ACTION AT THE CLIMAX OF SEASON THREE OF *STAR WARS: THE CLONE WARS*, *STAR WARS INSIDER* MET THE MAN WHO CREATED THE ROLE BACK IN 1977, PETER MAYHEW. INTERVIEW BY JONATHAN WILKINS

pads were in the wrong position, and that gave him a bigger neck. We took those out and it altered all of Chewie's stance and persona. Chewie became Chewie again, rather than just another Wookiee.

Was it tough working with the cutting-edge special effects on *Revenge of the Sith*?
Revenge of the Sith was a very different kind of *Star Wars* movie. I had done the first three movies with hardly any blue screen work but *Sith* was all blue screen! It was a completely different background. Things that should be there, aren't there! For example, in the council chamber, there were no other actors. It was just me on that particular set, and everything was marked out, so that we knew where people were sitting so that we could look that way or look the other way, whatever was needed. It worked.

Why do you think Chewie is such an enduring icon?
I think he's a big teddy bear and someone that could look after you if things started to go wrong. He's extremely loyal to certain people and yet he's quite capable of pulling his enemies' arms off and destroying stuff in a rage.
　　Chewie's fans see him in lots of different ways. For some people, he's

"I HAVE FRIENDS ALL OVER THE WORLD AS A RESULT OF PLAYING CHEWIE. THE FANS ARE ALWAYS SO KIND."

Top: Han meets Jabba (Declan Mulholland) as Peter Mayhew debuts the Chewie costume on the set of *A New Hope*. Left: Taking a break during filming for *The Empire Strikes Back*.

a teddy bear, for others he's a hero, because he and Han would go in and do things that only heroes would dare to do. A lot of fans love him because he's so good in a fight! I don't even think Darth Vader would have messed with him.
　　Wherever I go there will always be someone that will recognize me and come up and say hello. I have friends all over the world as a result of playing Chewie. The more conventions I do, the more I feel honored. Hopefully, I'm going to be able to carry on for a good number of years, traveling the world, and meeting the fans who are always so kind and wonderful.

Do you collect Chewie merchandise?
Wherever I go, whether it's a little convention or a big convention, there's always Chewie merchandise. I'm given drawings from kids, models from teenagers, and even original newspaper cuttings and art connected to Chewie. I've got a very large Chewbacca museum at home with six cabinets of Chewie stuff—from 23-inch dolls down to the three-inch dolls. We have a very interesting collection!

Did you keep any souvenirs from the movie set?
When we were making the original movie, nobody knew it was going to

Top and right: Behind the scenes with Peter in 2004 and 1976. Below left: With George Lucas on the blue screen set of Episode III.

I was sure you were going to say the *Millennium Falcon*!
Ah, yes! But they broke it up. The last time I saw the *Millennium Falcon,* it was in three pieces, and they got rid of it. Anyway, my back garden in England wouldn't be big enough for it. Sometimes people say, "Oh, wouldn't you want the costume?" My philosophy is that you don't take work clothes home. The folks at the Lucasfilm Archives have looked after the Chewbacca costumes really well.

It would have been a good thing to have on Halloween, wouldn't it?
Oh yeah, I would love to go out in it, but nobody would believe it was really me!

When you're not attending conventions, what do you do?
I've just written two books: *Growing Up Giant* and *My Favorite Giant*. The first one is a kids' book that I did to inspire every child that feels different. It's dedicated to one of the daughters of the founder of the 501st Legion, Katie Johnson. Katie died of cancer at age seven. So a part of the proceeds will go to Make-A-Wish Foundation. You can get both books directly from my website or through Barnes and Noble. ☮

be the big hit that it turned out to be. There were a couple of things, but it's too late now. I'd have liked the binders [handcuffs] that were used on Chewie in *A New Hope*. They played a fairly big part.

EXPANDED

Catch up with Peter at
www.petermayhew.com

UNIVERSE

WORLD EXCLUSIVE: *STAR WARS REBELS* **LAUNCH ISSUE!**

STAR WARS
INSIDER

EXCLUSIVE!
A NEW DAWN
Creating the Stunning
Rebels Prequel Novel!

DROID DESIGN!
Meet the Man who
Builds Real-life Droids!

ISSUE #152
US $7.99
CAN $9.99
OCTOBER 2014

TITAN

STAR WARS REBELS
MEET THE CREW OF THE *GHOST*!
THE REBELS: INTERVIEWED INSIDE!
SECRETS OF THE SHOW REVEALED!

7 25274 22493 7
5 2

VANESSA MARSHALL
HERA

ISSUE 152
OCTOBER 2014

Often, the stars of *Star Wars* are fans themselves. That is never more true than in the case of *Star Wars Rebels* voice actor, Vanessa Marshall, who portrays Hera in the show. As part of the promotion to launch the new show, we interviewed the entire cast in a special commemorative issue. Vanessa was so keen to read the article that she contacted our subscriptions team to order some extra copies. Now, I hold to a rule that if somebody is involved in the making of *Star Wars*, then they should get a free copy! After all, it's thanks to their efforts that there is a magazine in the first place. Vanessa, however, was having none of it. We did insist she get a free *Insider* T-shirt, and got her to agree to write an ongoing column about her *Star Wars* experiences in the magazine, entitled *Vanessa's View*.—**Jonathan Wilkins**

Vanessa Marshall was born on October 19, 1969. She is most active in voice-over roles for animated series, films and video games. She is the daughter of actress Joan Van Ark and reporter John Marshall. She began voice-over work after being discovered at a one woman show. Her roles include Black Widow in Avengers: Earth's Mightiest Heroes, Mary Jane Watson in The Spectacular Spider-Man, and Wonder Woman in Justice League. She most recently voiced the role of Gamora in the Guardians of the Galaxy animated series.

A LONG-STANDING *STAR WARS* FAN, VANESSA MARSHALL'S DREAM CAME TRUE WHEN SHE WAS CAST AS HERA SYNDULLA IN *STAR WARS REBELS*. INTERVIEW BY JONATHAN WILKINS

1 When were you first aware of *Star Wars*?
1977. I saw *A New Hope* with my cousins in Boulder, Colorado. It was essentially the first day of the rest of my life! I was hooked from the very first moment, when the Imperial Star Destroyer rumbled across the screen. It was *game on* from that point forward.

Recently, someone asked me, "What's the best film ever made?" I said, "Well, so far there are six of them!" I think the entire saga is the best story ever told.

2 Who is your favorite character?
Leia! George Lucas gave young women such a fantastic icon to emulate in terms of her confidence, her humor, and her hair! But running a close second is Ahsoka in *Star Wars: The Clone Wars*. I truly, *truly* love Ahsoka. I worry about her every day. I hope she's okay. Ashley Eckstein did such a great job! I'm all about Team Ahsoka!

Do you have a favorite *Star Wars* scene?
I have several. In *Revenge of the Sith* when Padmé says, "So this is how liberty dies, with thunderous applause." That gave me chills.

I also love the moment when Anakin asks Palpatine, "Is it possible to learn this power?" and Ian McDiarmid, savoring every single syllable replies, "Not... from a Jedi." It's just four simple words, but Ian's delivery made my blood run cold. Brilliant acting! And finally the scene in *The Clone Wars* when Ahsoka leaves Anakin. That moment just killed me. That silent fade to black still makes me cry.

Can you reveal something about yourself that will surprise *Star Wars* fans?
As much as I wanted to order Bo-Katan armor from Kevin Weir of the 501st SoCal Garrison, I decided to go with Hera cosplay instead! I was chatting with a lovely girl on Twitter from Twi'lek Paradise, and I asked her, "Could you make me green Lekku?" and she said "Absolutely!" She sent me the bill, and it was in Euros, so I said, "I'm sorry, did I miss something?" and she said, "Yes, I'm in Spain!" So I have exceptional lekku from España! Well worth the international shipping!

Where did you sign your first *Star Wars* autograph?
I think it may have been at a "May the Fourth Be With You" event this year. We were at the LA Children's Hospital to celebrate. Disney provided these really cool images of Hera with TIE fighters, and the kids lined up for autographs. It was really lovely. Just to watch the kids dance with Artoo-Detoo. They were so happy! Vader and Boba were there too! We all had fun. That was my first official signing.

3 Han Solo or Luke Skywalker?
For swagger? Han! For being a true hero? Luke! I love them both for different reasons. Han makes me laugh, and Luke makes me think. Although, Han *is* my favorite Black Series action figure!

4 See-Threepio or Artoo-Detoo?
I think Artoo. He's so dear. I have the foot-tall Artoo model. When you say "Dance, Artoo!" the Cantina theme plays. This is what I do with my Friday nights!

5 Darth Vader or Darth Maul?
Darth Vader. Vader's arc is the richest one for me. He scares me to death. When I go to any of the 501st events, and I hear the sound of him breathing nearby, I can barely take it! It's terrifying. But when you know what kind of deep sorrow fuels his agenda, he becomes one of the most complex characters in all entertainment. Even though I fear Vader, I have a fondness for Anakin. It was so satisfying to see him ultimately return to his son. That redemption inspires me. Daily. ☻

STAR WARS

INSIDER

ROYAL REBEL!
Princess Leia stars
in amazing new tale

EXCLUSIVE!
GEORGE LUCAS
on the strange
Star Wars novel
you never saw!

ISSUE 145
NOV/DEC 2013
U.S. $7.99
Can $9.99
Please display until December 09 2013

TITAN

VICTIM OR VILLAIN?

IS THIS SITH LORD *STAR WARS'* GREATEST HERO?

DARTH VADER: VICTIM OR VILLAIN?

ISSUE 145
NOVEMBER/DECEMBER 2013

As the *Star Wars* saga continued beyond the original movie, it naturally evolved. Darth Vader was no longer the all-evil figure he seemed to be. I felt it was time to look at whether Vader, or indeed Anakin Skywalker, was a victim or villain, and invited some of the great *Star Wars* authors, whose work for Del Rey has entertained and enthralled readers for over 20 years, to contribute. They all offered fascinating insight and amazing ideas. I still think Timothy Zahn's "What if Vader had survived at the end of *Return of the Jedi*?" would make a great book.—**Jonathan Wilkins**

Timothy Zahn reignited the literary Star Wars *universe with the best-selling* Thrawn Trilogy (Heir to the Empire, Dark Force Rising, *and* The Last Command). *Zahn also wrote* Specter of the Past, Vision of the Future, Survivor's Quest, Outbound Flight, Allegiance, Choices of One *and* Scoundrels.

Aaron Allston wrote 13 Star Wars *novels, and several short stories. His oeuvre includes* X-Wing: Starfighters of Adumar, *three of the nine-book* Legacy of the Force *series, followed by three of the nine-book* Fate of the Jedi *series and* X-Wing: Mercy Kill.

John Jackson Miller's most notable works are the Knights of the Old Republic *and* Knight Errant *comic series. His novel,* Kenobi, *was one of the last of the Expanded Universe stories prior to their rebranding as Legends, while 2014's* A New Dawn *was the first book of the new canon.*

Christie Golden's award-winning novels include three stunning entries in the Fate of the Jedi *series (*Omen, Allies, *and* Acension). *As well as writing four short stories, Golden also wrote the new canon novel,* Dark Disciple, *using unfilmed scripts from the* Star Wars: The Clone Wars *TV series.*

Michael Reaves co-wrote "Tail of the Roon Comets," an episode of the Star Wars: Droids *animated television series. He also wrote the* Star Wars: Ewoks *episodes entitled "The Raich" and "Hard Sell." His novels include* Darth Maul: Shadow Hunter *and the* Coruscant Nights *trilogy.*

Maya Kaathryn Bohnhoff is the co-author of the novel Shadow Games *and later* The Last Jedi *with Michael Reaves. She also co-wrote (uncredited) the 2009 novel* Coruscant Nights III: Patterns of Force *with Reaves.*

Douglas Wheatley has provided the art for Star Wars *comic books, including* Star Wars: Empire, Star Wars: Republic, *and the adaptation of* Revenge of the Sith.

Kevin Hearne's first entry in the Star Wars *canon is the Luke Skywalker adventure,* Heir to the Jedi.

Ryder Windham has written a prolific amount of Star Wars *titles, including junior novelizations of the original trilogy, and eight Episode I adventures.*

Joe Schreiber is best known for bringing horror to the Star Wars *universe with the novels* Death Troopers *and* Red Harvest. *His suspenseful 2014 novel,* Maul Lockdown, *saw the Zabrak Sith warrior incarcerated!*

Jason Fry has authored short stories and the young readers' novel The Clone Wars: Darth Maul: Shadow Conspiracy. *He has also contributed to a number of books tied in to* Star Wars: The Force Awakens.

Darth Vader art by Brian Rood

Darth Vader

VICTIM OR VILLAIN?

IT'S BEEN 30 YEARS SINCE DARTH VADER DIED ABOARD THE DEATH STAR. WE ASKED SOME TOP *STAR WARS* CREATORS IF THE DARK LORD IS AS EVIL AS HE SEEMS—OR IF VADER IS, IN FACT, THE TRUE HERO OF THE *STAR WARS* SAGA...

⊛ THE EXPERTS! /////

TIMOTHY ZAHN — Author of the first post-*Return of the Jedi* novel, *Heir to the Empire,* and more recently the instant classic, *Scoundrels*

AARON ALLSTON — Author of the acclaimed X-Wing series and co-author of the Fate of the Jedi novels

JOHN JACKSON MILLER — Author of *Knights of the Old Republic*, *Knight Errant* and the current smash, *Kenobi*

CHRISTIE GOLDEN — Co-author of the Fate of the Jedi series

MICHAEL REAVES — Author of several *Star Wars* novels, including *Darth Maul: Shadow Hunter*, and the co-authored *Death Star* and *The Last Jedi*

MAYA KAATHRYN BOHNHOFF — Co-author of *Shadow Games* and *The Last Jedi*

DOUGLAS WHEATLEY — Artist behind the comic book adaptation of *Revenge of the Sith* and *Star Wars: Purge*

KEVIN HEARNE — Author of the upcoming yet-to-be titled installment in the *Star Wars: Empire* and *Rebellion* series

RYDER WINDHAM – Author of over 50 *Star Wars* books, including *Star Wars: Death Star Owner's Technical Manual*

JOE SCHREIBER — Author of *Star Wars: Death Troopers*, *Star Wars: Red Harvest*, and *Star Wars: Maul: Lockdown*.

JASON FRY – The author of numerous reference books and popular titles for younger readers.

TIMOTHY ZAHN

He's certainly a victim, in as much as he was enslaved as a child, fought through a terrible war, and was manipulated by pretty much everyone he held dear (though to be fair, sometimes that manipulation wasn't deliberate). However, none of that relieves him of the responsibility to make the right moral decisions. His past may have made his perspective murkier and those decisions more difficult, but he still must accept accountability for his actions.

AARON ALLSTON

He's both. Clearly, circumstances helped turn him toward a tragic destiny. But he also made "bad guy" decisions. He found and embraced justifications for genuinely evil actions. (He may have felt he was being altruistic in his desire to save Shmi, then Padmé, but it was actually selfishness on his part, an unwillingness to suffer loss, that led to outrage after outrage.) Regardless of the amount of sympathy his circumstances generate for him, that's a villainous trait.

JOHN JACKSON MILLER

I think he's definitely responsible for many of the things that went wrong in his life. After his release from the bondage of slavery, he became convinced of his own uniqueness and infallibility—a point of view that, regrettably, I think the Jedi Order encouraged, wittingly or not. A lot of my writings on the Order—particularly in the *Knights of the Old Republic* graphic novels—get into how hubris is the Jedi's great failing. It's hard to be set above all other mortals without losing perspective. But while some other Jedi worked very hard to cope with that problem, Anakin rarely tried to restrain himself, usually taking the easiest path his powers made available to him. Because he could do something, he often did—and this is what led to lapses in judgment when tragic circumstances did arise, such as the Tusken Raiders kidnapping his mother.

His grief and anger then was natural

and human—but his decision to go out alone lay rooted in his arrogance: His confidence in his own powers and his own ability to set things right. Had he recognized the danger his emotionally compromised state represented and sought the help of Padmé or others, it might have resulted in a much different end. But that wasn't Anakin's way.

CHRISTIE GOLDEN

I have to say "None of the above" or more precisely: a combination of both. I think that his actions were the result of a unique combination of personality, history, and circumstances. Others with Anakin's gifts might well have succumbed to the dark side sooner; still, others would have been able to resist its seduction. He was flawed, as all beings are flawed, and in such a fashion that he made choices that led, inexorably, to his fall. Not a victim—but not an evil person either.

MICHAEL REAVES

Both. We don't know much about his years in the Jedi Temple, but we can assume, from what we've learned of the way the rest of the younglings and Padawans

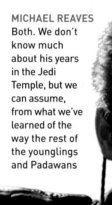

were treated, that they were all pretty much victims of benign neglect and indifference. This doesn't mean that their needs weren't met, or that they weren't treated with respect, even kindness and fondness, but they seem to be treated that way largely as a group. Despite the pairing of Jedi Knight and Padawan, there was little attention given to individuation. Puberty no doubt complicated things to a much bigger degree, and so the kids were largely left to figure out themselves how to deal with each other. That said, it's also known that Anakin Skywalker was by temperament a loner, who didn't play well with others.

> ## "Anakin Skywalker was by temperment a loner, who didn't play well with others." —Michael Reaves

MAYA KAATHRYN BOHNHOFF

He's both. In any life, a person is given a set of circumstances which they react to. Anakin Skywalker's circumstances—from his childhood as a slave, to the loss of his mother—were tragic, but his reactions to these things were his choice. His response to most things that ran counter to his wishes was anger, and he looked for someone to blame for his situation. Once a person or group was targeted for blame, Anakin set out with single-minded will to destroy them. Tusken Raiders, Jedi (in the *Coruscant Nights* books, Jax Pavan, a fellow Jedi), even the woman he supposedly loved were blamed and targeted for destruction.

And that's what makes Darth Vader a "bad guy"—his penchant for acting selfishly, driven by anger, and then blaming the disastrous results on someone else. This,

oddly, makes him a sort of darker version of Han "Not My Fault" Solo—whose childhood was about as unpleasant as Anakin's. The difference—Han's deft dodging of fault did not cause him to foist blame onto someone else or to try to wipe out those he felt were responsible for his misery. Anakin ever and always made his anger, misery, and heartbreak someone else's fault.

DOUGLAS WHEATLEY

Tragic circumstance. Anakin was being manipulated by both the Sith and the Jedi, caught in the middle of a galactic tug of war for power and there was incredible pressure on him due to his status "as the one who would bring balance to the Force."

RYDER WINDHAM

I think most *Star Wars* fans would agree that Anakin became Darth Vader by way of

circumstances, Palpatine's manipulations, and his own decisions.

KEVIN HEARNE

He's a truly bad guy in my view. Many other people lose their mothers and wives, but don't conclude that the only way to make it all better is to kill lots of people. We can feel his pain—anybody who's lost someone close to them has an idea of the emotions he's feeling—but we can't excuse him for his choices. He embraced the dark side.

JOE SCHREIBER

It's a fascinating and relevant question. I don't know how much anybody else is commenting on the issue, but I'm pretty sure he falls soundly on the "villain" side of the fence. The whole "victim of tragic circumstance" angle isn't particularly helpful or compelling once we realize that we all carry a deep seed of villainy inside us—and viewing ourselves solely in the context of victims of worldly circumstance is dangerously close to self-pity. On the positive side, I'd like to believe that nobody (even Vader himself) is beyond the ultimate reach of forgiveness, redemption... dare I say, grace?

Who is really to blame for the tragedy of Darth Vader? Anakin, Obi-Wan Kenobi, the Jedi, or Palpatine?

TIMOTHY ZAHN

I think there's more than enough blame to go around. The Jedi should have realized they were forcing Anakin into a position where he felt he was betraying a friend and they should have found a different approach. Obi-Wan should have made it clear to Anakin that if his investigation showed that Palpatine wasn't scheming to take over the Republic, the Council would back off. Palpatine shouldn't have—never mind; Palpatine was trying to manipulate him.

And Anakin himself... well, in retrospect he probably should have reached out to the people he still trusted, Padmé and Obi-Wan, and expressed his fears and anger. Maybe it would have provided some fresh perspective and helpful advice. Unfortunately, by the time he got the Council's marching orders, it was probably too late for him to even consider doing something like that.

AARON ALLSTON

They all are. I suspect that Anakin lacked empathy— perhaps as a persistent characteristic of his fear of loss. He might not wish to connect emotionally with someone he might/ must ultimately lose. But lack of empathy causes people to do cruel things without thought or reservation. Not every Tusken Raider Anakin killed was necessarily guilty of harming Shmi... but they all ended up identically dead.

Obi-Wan was a parent surrogate for Anakin, but was terrible at it. He tried to instruct Anakin in the austere, objective Jedi way, but didn't notice that Anakin did not have a foundation of humanity on which a conscience and good decision-making are based. Obi-Wan looked on Anakin as a brother... but Anakin needed a father. And there was no father.

The Jedi of that era were a monastic order made up of people who had largely left the world of passions and other lesser concerns behind. They were, therefore, unprepared to deal with, to guide, someone who was deeply mired in that world.

And Palpatine was just being Palpatine. It was in his nature to isolate, to twist, and to corrupt. Anakin didn't stand a chance.

So they were all responsible. But Anakin was ultimately responsible, because at every stage of his process of corruption, he could have chosen to say "enough"—to suffer loss or even to die rather than to perpetuate the tragedy he was living.

JOHN JACKSON MILLER

Anakin. Palpatine put temptations in his way—and the Jedi did, too. Not just in training him; by accepting him into their order, they gave him great influence over others, which he too happily accepted. So neither is faultless, although the Jedi's problem was negligence, compared to Palpatine's malice. But Anakin is ultimately the one who acted, here. He could have turned back.

The *Kenobi* novel finds Obi-Wan asking this same question, by the way—worrying over what his culpability was, and whether he could have done anything different. It also shows Obi-Wan giving others who have gone wrong every chance to turn back before it's too late. He cannot save someone who won't be saved, but he refuses to let it happen solely on account of his not lending help and the opportunity at every turn.

CHRISTIE GOLDEN

I think Sidious/Palpatine and Anakin were co-creators in what was to become Darth Vader. Anakin would not have fallen without the specific temptations offered by Palpatine; Sidious would not have been able to corrupt Anakin if Anakin were not flawed in exactly that particular manner.

MAYA KAATHRYN BOHNHOFF

No matter how I look at it, I find it hard to blame Obi-Wan or the Jedi. Of course, they could have saved everyone a lot of grief if they'd bought Anakin's mom out of slavery, too, but that was a writer's decision, not a natural outcome of anything in the world or the characters. The Jedi clearly had enough material resources to free Mom; they didn't because her death would later serve as a catalyst for Anakin's turning to the dark side,

which is why I say that it was a writer's decision, not a character's decision.

So rather than step beyond the proscenium (or the silver screen, in this case), I'd say the Jedi aren't "to blame." Did they keep Anakin from doing or having what he wanted? Yeah, they did. But what he wanted wasn't necessarily good for anyone—not even Anakin Skywalker. Padmé also tried to keep Anakin from doing things that were ill-conceived, but it's hard to blame her for anything but exercising poor judgment in choosing a mate.

So, who's to blame? I think the parties most responsible for Anakin becoming Darth Vader are Anakin himself and Palpatine. Whatever negative effect the Jedi (including Obi-Wan) had on Anakin, it was not intentional cruelty or motivated by selfishness. Palpatine, on the other hand, manipulated Anakin (and everyone else around him) with nothing but selfish and cruel intent. In fact, from Palpatine's perspective, this is not about blame at all, but about who gets to take credit for crafting Darth Vader from the raw clay of Anakin Skywalker.

DOUGLAS WHEATLEY
The Jedi, and Sidious, had a significant influence on Anakin. Yoda mentions in Episode III that the Jedi were not meant to be generals in a war and are acting

outside of their former roles in the galaxy and that this path is a dangerous one. Anakin pleads with Mace Windu to bring Palpatine to trial, clearly doing his best to adhere to the Jedi principles. Master Windu answers Anakin during his struggle with Palpatine, telling him that "he is too dangerous to remain alive," which is exactly what Palpatine said to Anakin during his battle with Count Dooku. Coincidence, or was this an indication that the Jedi Order

had lost their focus, lost their way due to the manipulation of the Sith and were out of balance with the Force?

That said, Anakin made his own decisions, and what is a man who can't be measured by his own actions? Luke made a different decision under similar circumstances, and in that decision, he helped to restore his father... Anakin made Darth Vader tragic.

RYDER WINDHAM
It's all George Lucas's fault. Okay, seriously, many characters played significant roles in shaping Anakin for better or worse, everyone from Tatooine slavers and Tusken Raiders to the Jedi and Padmé Amidala. It's easy to blame Sidious/Palpatine for being the villain who lured Anakin to the dark side, but consider that Anakin never would have met Palpatine if Qui-Gon Jinn had just left him on Tatooine. Everyone who had an emotional impact on Anakin could be blamed for some part in his tragedy.

KEVIN HEARNE
Anakin can blame no one but himself. We may not get to choose the circumstances of our lives, but we are always free to choose how to react. Luke reacts to the trap Admiral Ackbar so helpfully pointed out by rejecting fear and anger; Anakin reacts to his personal tragedies with unholy killing sprees.

> **"Obi-Wan looked on Anakin as a brother... but Anakin needed a father."** —Aaron Allston

TIMOTHY ZAHN

I think redemption is always possible. In Anakin's case, I would argue that he was officially redeemed, at least as far as the Force was concerned (however the Force judges these things), since he was back to being a Jedi in Luke's spirit vision on Endor.

However, redemption doesn't mean that the consequences of his actions are simply wiped clean. Had he survived Endor, there would necessarily have been a trial, where Vader would have been called to account for his actions. On some things he could plead severe emotional stress (the killing of the Tusken Raiders) or deliberate manipulation of the facts (the killing of a clearly berserk Mace Windu as he tried to assassinate the Chancellor). Others, like the slaughter of the younglings, aren't so easily dismissed.

Had he survived, perhaps we'd have seen the pitiable image of Vader, humbly and uncomplainingly, accepting execution, imprisonment, or exile. Or maybe he would have spent the rest of his life traveling the galaxy, going to the families of each of his victims to confess his actions and ask their forgiveness. A broken, haunted, but determined man, alone on his final mission....

AARON ALLSTON

I think every author will have his or her own answer as to whether Vader should have been redeemable. If I were in charge of the *Star Wars* universe, I'd say no—I'd say that saving Luke at the end was just one more example of Anakin being unwilling to experience loss, that no actual redemption took place.

But it's not my universe. It is, or at least was, George Lucas', and he decided long ago that Anakin was redeemable, and that he was redeemed. I accept that. So, yes, Anakin/Vader was redeemed. Period.

Still, to this day, when people tell me, "Luke redeemed Darth Vader," I ask in turn, "Yeah? What did Luke get for him?"

JOHN JACKSON MILLER

I don't think he can completely redeem himself, but that ties into my sense of what the term means. And it means different things in different philosophies. Some believe that the simple act of rejecting temptation brings on redemption; others demand more. I wouldn't try to suggest which one should apply: If anything, we'd want to know what the Jedi view on redemption is.

But if you stick to the classical English definition of the word, redemption is a "purchasing back"—in this case, from captivity. Under this thinking, it's actually Luke whose selfless act to reach Anakin redeems him and frees his father from the captivity of evil. That's the redemption that leaves Vader free to act, and he chooses the side of right. A religious person might say Luke redeemed Vader so that he could begin his atonement—a process that began with overthrowing the Emperor.

JASON FRY ON DARTH VADER

"Like all villains who are more than cardboard, Vader's both villain and victim. He's a mass-murderer on an unimaginable scale, but we can see how he got there—he was used and led astray (by both the Sith and the Jedi) and then lashed out in a fury and made awful choices. Which is interesting to me on a character level, but also because it points to the deep strangeness that's everywhere in *Star Wars*, if you care to look. Like all great mythic journeys, *Star Wars* offers iconic storytelling and classic character roles along with a shadowy, queasy ambiguity. You wouldn't set out to create a saga whose central character is an emotionally stunted war criminal who arose from a virgin birth, but here we are—and it's a fascinating place to be."

> **"Had he survived, perhaps we'd have seen the pitiable image of Vader humbly and uncomplainingly accepting execution, imprisonment, or exile."**
> —Timothy Zahn

Had Anakin lived longer, I'd expect his atonement would've continued until the day he died. Nothing he would ever be able to do would put things right, but precisely balancing the ledger isn't what atonement's about. This is something *Kenobi* touches on: You can't undo the past. Your life, at that point, is about what you can do for the future.

CHRISTIE GOLDEN

I think so. A truly remorseful heart must be forgiven by something as benevolent and loving as the light side of the Force. And it could be argued that in saving Luke, who went on to do so much for the galaxy, Vader even made reparation.

MAYA KAATHRYN BOHNHOFF

I suppose the answer to this depends on one's view of the universe and the nature of the Force. In my more charitable moments, I understand the idea at the core of real-world religion that redemption is possible for anyone who

seeks it and is willing to sacrifice themselves to undo or at least redress the evil they've done.

In that view, the soul that is Anakin Skywalker can be redeemed if he comes to a realization of the full enormity of his actions, regrets them to the bottom of his soul, perhaps begs forgiveness of the appropriate parties, and does whatever he can to redress those wrongs. In other words, if there's a sea-change in his purpose: Instead of pursuing the dark goal of enslaving others, he ultimately helps free them, even at the price of his own mortal life.

Now, it could be argued that he didn't do enough, but destroying Palpatine and saving the one person he knew was capable of rekindling the Jedi Order really accomplished a great deal. It changed the flow of history and saved the galaxy from certain enslavement. Besides, Anakin is now a Force spirit, so who knows the amount of good he might accomplish. No, really, who knows?

Left: The tragic consequences of Anakin's fall from grace as the Jedi are brutally extinguished.

Above left: Anakin redeemed... but can he be forgiven?

Above right: Darth Vader forces Leia to watch the destruction of her home planet and her people.

Of course, this raises the question: in the Galaxy Far, Far Away, who decides whether Vader's turnaround and sacrifice is enough to redeem him? And that, in turn, takes us back to the beginning of my answer—it depends on one's view of the universe and the nature of the Force.

KEVIN HEARNE

I don't think so. Destroying the Emperor wasn't noble of Vader. In fact, that "rebellion" merely followed the pattern he had already established: Threaten or harm someone close to him, and he will slay you.

DOUGLAS WHEATLEY

Vader made a crucial decision to destroy the Emperor; he saw his error and recognized what needed to be done and knowingly sacrificed himself. In the end, he stepped over the median from dark to light, and breathed his last breath as a free man.

In our society, we will punish a person for a past wrong, regardless of how that person conducts themselves in the present. He must pay his debt to society, right? This scenario begs the question; what is the result that we as a people are after – punishment or a change of character? I think for George, in his galaxy, decided change was enough for redemption.

RYDER WINDHAM

Because Anakin's spiritual form appears alongside the spirits of Obi-Wan and Yoda at the end of *Return of the Jedi*, we can assume he redeemed himself by some Jedi standard. But you're essentially asking if Vader deserved to be redeemed. Consider the scope of Vader's atrocities, then ask: Even though he ultimately chose to sacrifice himself to kill the Emperor and save his own son, do you forgive him? And do you think a reasonable judge and jury would let him walk? ☻

EXPANDED

Special thanks to Erich Schoeneweiss, Shelly Shapiro, and Frank Parisi for their assistance in preparing this article.

UNIVERSE